The Aspie College, Work & Travel Survival Guide

By J.D. Kraus

BOONE COUNTY PUBLIC LIBRARY
BURLINGTON, KY 41005
www.bcpl.org

The Aspie College, Work & Travel Survival Guide

All marketing and publishing rights guaranteed to and reserved by:

FUTURE HORIZONS INC.

721 W Abram St, Arlington, TX 76013

800-489-0727 (toll free)

817-277-0727 (local)

817-277-2270 (fax)

E-mail: *info@fhautism.com*

www.fhautism.com

ISBN: 9781941765128

Dedication

In memory of my mother, the most compassionate
and strongest willed person in my life.

Contents

Prologue:

This Book Is for Whom?

Before answering this question, I have a few matters to address. I am not a psychologist, a therapist or a doctor. I am a young adult who has been diagnosed with Asperger's syndrome, also called AS. Asperger's is on the autistic spectrum. As an adult with AS, I have ventured into the world beyond the high school setting. In my life, I have faced my ups and downs, the joys and frustrations, and the successes and failures. Everything I share with you is from my experience.

The first book I wrote, *The Aspie Teen's Survival Guide*, was centered on helping elementary through high-school-aged individuals on the autistic spectrum. The book offered additional advice for parents with AS children. This book serves as a sequel of sorts. Here I will focus on the topics concerning life after high school, including but not limited to higher education, employment, and traveling.

My mission is to help guide persons with autism-related disorders into becoming young adults. The possibilities are limitless for them, and it can be incredibly intimidating, especially for Aspies who are most comfortable in a structured world. Unfortunately, life beyond high school is anything but structured.

I cannot tell you what your life will be like after high school; only you can choose your path. What I can do is help guide you on how to prepare and handle a variety of situations you might face. Take comfort in knowing that many people with autism have found success. Some have even gone on to become famous.

Now, you may wonder how you can find your place in this world after leaving high school. I, for one, totally loathed junior high and high school. I was often bullied and labeled as a "freak." Classmates can be mean-spirited. Down the road, it is likely you will encounter some unpleasant people, but things can get better. Outside general education, most people will not go out of their way to bully or torment you. In fact, if you go on to college or the employment world, you will find that a lot of people are actually quite open-minded.

Another great thing you'll find beyond high school is the number of possibilities you have. You now have the opportunity to do what you want to achieve. You can join a club, enroll full-time at a non-profit organization, learn a new trade or write a book (as in my case!). After high school is the ideal time to pursue your life's objectives. Be aware that it does take time to achieve goals, especially long-term ones. It is a process. You have to stay dedicated and motivated.

Who Else Should Read This Book? Why?

While my main objective is to help guide young persons with autism-related disorders as well as offer candid advice to parents with

Aspie children, this book is not just restricted to these specific audiences. I encourage people not on the autistic spectrum to pick up this book, specifically young individuals that are questioning their next step in life. As I previously stated, I cannot tell you what career to go after. What I can prepare you for are the different processes and steps it takes to enroll in universities and technical schools, to get a job, and to plan for travel.

Sadly, most high schools do not train their students very well for the real world or higher education. School and the work world are very different. High school is nothing like college, and college is vastly different from the workplace.

For parents with children on the autism spectrum, there is little guidance for me to offer. From kindergarten to high school, my parents played a very active role in my school success, whether it was with homework, projects, faculty meetings, construction of my IEP, or even selection of my teachers for the following class year. Such chances to provide assistance are significantly fewer in college and the employment world. This is the part of your AS child's life in which she will be on her own. The purpose of college is to prepare young people to think on their own and acquire a set of skills. Work is an environment where individuals learn to fit in with others and provide a livelihood.

For parents, even though your AS son is of legal age, it does not mean he is entirely ready for what lies ahead. There are still things you can do to assist him in this new phase in life, but you will have to take a passenger seat in the journey. Your child is the driver. The most important thing you can do for him is offer support. The freshman year of college and the first year of work are often the most difficult times. Stress and meltdowns can occur, so be there for him.

How Is This Book Organized?

Much of my focus will be on the transition from high school to college, a critical time that calls for a lot of exploring and guidance. The steps involving enrollment at an educational institution, for example, are meticulous and difficult.

The next big portion of this book will explain the different kinds of colleges (namely community colleges, technical schools, and universities) and what to anticipate from them, such as teachers, assignments, campus life, and costs. I will also go into detail about living on campus versus daily commuting as well as developing time management skills and the procedures to prepare for graduation.

Following that section, I will cover aspects of job hunting and employment, such as where to apply on-line, how to build contacts, write a resumé, prepare for job interviews, etc.

Then, I will share some miscellaneous chapters on how to handle a variety of emergency situations (i.e., auto accidents, injury, ill health, and family tragedy) and traveling domestically and internationally. My hope is that this book is resourceful to you and your family and will be quite beneficial for young AS adults.

Chapter 1

To Go to College or Not?

Of course, I cannot answer this question for you. Ultimately, this is your choice. No one can force you to attend a university, and college is not for everyone, but it can also be a great experience for many. There are certain things you need to consider when making this decision. *1)* How much time are you willing to devote to studying before you start your career? *2)* What degree do you think will be the most beneficial in your career plans? *3)* Will a college education be valuable to your career?

The answer to the first question was easy for me, because I found a community college that offered an associate's degree with an option to transfer into a bachelor program. The second question was answered for me when I found a program that addressed my particular interests. As an Aspie, my interests were in video and animation. Yours might be very different from mine; find a program that suits your interests.

In addressing whether college would be beneficial to my career, I considered the fact that my family knew the value of a college education. My mother, who advocated for me through high school, shared with me her experiences in college. She started out in a two-year program and then transferred to a bachelor program. I followed a similar path. Note to Aspie students: talk to your family for guidance when making your decisions regarding college.

You may find that a community college is less expensive than a four-year university.

In my case, the cost was about one half of a four-year bachelor program. This can be helpful, since college tuition can be pretty scary for both students and parents who may bear the costs.

Another matter that some college students face is whether their course of study is relevant to their intended careers. While college teaches theory, principles and technical attributes, it does not often cover skills that are learned from hardened experience like communication, time management and organization. No professor can teach a student how he should manage his time or complete his assignments in a timely fashion.

Another thing to consider about college is that it can be challenging. During my freshman year, I had to take a graphic design course. At first, I loved the class. It was a think-outside-the-box, do-whatever-you-want kind of class. By the third week, though, I was pummeled by my teacher's critique on one of my assignments and basically said my work was not good enough.

2

For the remainder of the term, I struggled to please my professor with each assignment. During my time in that class, I took the teacher's criticisms personally. Looking back now, I realize that my professor was just pushing me to improve my capabilities as a designer. I survived the class and did much better than I had anticipated. Other students weren't as lucky, and several of them dropped the course.

This experience shows the importance of having self-motivation. Many students don't feel motivated to progress in their degree, especially those who are registered in a program that is not the right fit. Keep in mind that there is a chance you may end up in a different career than you initially expected.

The Enlightening Truths of Getting a Degree

There is a belief that the more college education you receive, the more money you will earn in the work world. While this idea seems sound, it is not entirely true. Some individuals who have no college experience go on to become very successful. However, it's unlikely that you will make it big in the world without knowledge, experience or education. This is why you need some form of extended education and/or experience.

A college degree looks great on a resumé. It proves to potential employers that you have gone on after high school to acquire knowledge, and a degree shows you can commit to something and complete it. In addition, getting a degree opens doors for more opportunities. Many businesses today set higher education as a hiring requirement, so if you submit your application to a company without a degree, it may very well end up in the hiring manager's wastebasket.

As an individual with Asperger's, college has taught me two important lessons. College helped me find what I really wanted to do. In my late high school to early college years, I thought I wanted to be an animator. By my junior year in college, my gears shifted towards video production. In this way, college showed me what I was good at.

As an animator, I have trouble imagining a three-dimensional figure on a two-dimensional plane. It is very hard for me to achieve the task of depicting a cartoon character walking convincingly. However, I can write, plan out, and execute a video with very little trouble. It took me several years to figure out my true talents; college gives you that chance to discover your skills. Furthermore, college helped me build some connections.

Fellow students, faculty members and internship opportunities are three components that can help build your network. Doing well in college and bonding with both colleagues and professors may fare well in your future. I have learned that professors make excellent references for job hunting. Befriending classmates can open doors to paid gigs and even full-time jobs. Most of the time, finding your dream job comes down to who you know. Such connections have aided me in my media career. One connection presented the opportunity for me to participate in a feature length film, and another led to a broadcast credit on a television show.

It's Your Decision

I know I have mentioned this before, but going to college (or not) is entirely your choice. A desired career is a long-term goal. In my freshman year of college, one of my professors had the class fill out a packet with a series of questions like, "Where do you see yourself in five years?" "What are you talents?" and "What are your interests?"

I remember sitting at a table, pencil in hand, thinking, *Really? My professor is making me answer these silly questions for homework?* To get an easy A, I completed the assignment quickly, even if all my answers seemed unrealistic. For the following week, the next class assignment was to set up an appointment with our teacher to discuss our career goals. The meeting proved a rather interesting experience. The professor had read through my packet and made notes to my answers.

He said, "Your goals are reachable. You can become an award-winning filmmaker."

I felt embarrassed and a little shocked. *Was he being serious?* I wondered. I dared ask him that question. He replied, "Yes, if you put your mind to it, you can do anything. You're a good student. You have much to offer."

This meeting proved to be one of the most important ones I have ever had in my college experience. Since that day, I have held on to his words and used them as a guide for all my projects. You not only have to keep your goals both reachable and feasible, but you also need to know what it takes to accomplish them. Deciding to be a self-made billionaire is only a dream unless you figure out how you can obtain

5

such an objective. College and work can both be stepping stones on your path.

Notes to Parents: Your Part

I stated in the beginning of this book that parents will play more of a secondary role versus a primary one after high school. At this particular point in time in the life of your AS child, I strongly recommend that you sit down and talk with him. On many occasions during my high school years, my parents would ask the question, "So, what do you want to do when you get out of school?" My answer was always, "To get into movies."

However, I was not entirely sure what to do in the film industry. By my senior year in high school, my parents had invited me to participate in a discussion in our living room. We talked for at least an hour, going over school options. We spoke about which colleges to look into, how tuition will be handled, possible scholarships from my vocational school, distance from home, housing, food, and a whole lot more factors that could add another ten or so pages of discussion to this book. By the end of the talk, we came up with a game plan and several backup ones in case the first option didn't pan out.

This conversation can be one of the most important ones you have with your AS child. I cannot imagine the anxiety you might be feeling with regard to her future and the questions running through your mind. Will she go to college? Will she do well there? Should she stay home and seek employment nearby? What will she do when we're gone?

Whatever you and your AS teen decide to do, this should not be a terrifying experience for either of you. The journey into adulthood should be a fun experience. Even though I did not have a career fully imagined or planned, my excitement from getting out of high school was at full throttle.

Your AS child should not be afraid of the world outside his home. I know that may sound easier said than done because the transition from a conventional high school to a university is tough, but with patience and a little guidance, this transition can be worked out. Success takes effort, but it is worthwhile.

During one of our many conversations, my mother told me, "College is the place where you can find yourself." That statement couldn't be any truer. From my experience as an individual with Asperger's, higher education has been one of the best things to ever happen to me. I have been able to make friends and find interest in a line of work that I'm currently pursuing.

College could very well be the place where your AS child needs to go. Talk over the options available for him and make a decision together. If time permits, do not wait until his senior year to discuss his future. This could be too late for college registration and college-readiness tests. However, if you do miss the deadline, you might be able to work out another strategy. Remember, students don't always enroll in college immediately after high school. For example, my father did not get his college degree until I was born.

Chapter 2

Preparing for College

As a teenager with Asperger's syndrome, enrolling in a university was the least of my worries. My priorities were to hit the gym five times a week, battle acne, and play video games. Life as a teenager was a day-to-day project for me; I worried only about the present and not the future. It was not until my junior year that I realized there was so much more I could do in order to prepare for my future. High school only lasts for a few years. After that, poof, it's gone.

There is no rulebook of what to accomplish in order to secure a place in college. But there are several factors you might want to consider when pursuing higher education. While you're still a high school student, there is much you can do to prepare yourself, should you ultimately choose to enroll in a university. I suggest not waiting until the final two years of secondary education. Get a jump on your future.

What Do Colleges Look for in Students?

I originally thought that colleges were only interested in grades. Yes, a high GPA is an important factor for college enrollment. However, schools actually desire a variety of characteristics in their potential candidates:

College-Readiness Test Scores. Not to force a stress magnet on you, but the ACT and SAT play a big part in college admissions. Four-year colleges often require a student to take either the ACT or SAT, or both. I will go into further detail about these tests and how to prepare for them later on in the chapter.

Community Service. My school required all students to complete seventy-five hours of community service, which were due upon graduation. Originally, I groaned at the idea of community service. Being an Aspie, I limited my activities to my particular interests, and I felt uncomfortable doing new things. In an attempt to fulfill the service requirements, I volunteered at my mother's place of work, which happened to be a hospital. My mother introduced me to the volunteer coordinator, who helped me transition into this new environment. The first couple of days were rough, but I eventually adapted.

Organizations. On any college application, there is a section that lists organizations or clubs I participated in as a high school student. I always left that part blank. With Asperger's, I never really found an interest in socializing with other people. Thus, I never joined any clubs or organizations.

But in college, I learned that school organizations are some of the best campus activities. There is a larger variety of clubs and activities at college than there is in high school. As a result, I found several that were within my areas of interest.

Participation in organizations isn't always school-related. If you find interest in an outside club like a writer's group or something athletic-oriented, give it a try while you are still in high school. I recommend participating only in clubs that interest you.

Work outside of School. Balancing both work and school is incredibly demanding. Depending on the job, it could interfere with your school schedule. My parents always instilled in me the idea that education comes first, so I never worked while I was registered as a student. As a person with Asperger's syndrome, I have difficulty handling several different tasks at once. Work in addition to education would have been too hard for me to handle, especially during my teenage years. However, summer vacation could be an opportune time for me to earn some money. Like with school organizations, only consider this option if you find a position that interests you.

Choose this route only if you know you can do it.

Now, I am not implying that you must do everything listed to receive college admission. School, work, community service, and extracurricular activities add up to a lot of time invested in your future. If you have the time to do so, try to fit in some meaningful extracurricular activities outside the narrow interests of your home life. Extra side work will keep your mind busy and can help you achieve an extra sense of accomplishment.

During high school, I joined a local fitness club. Even though I chose not to participate in group-related activities, I was out of the house and in public. These fitness activities continued to be part of my life through college and into adulthood.

One last thing that may help boost your candidacy for college enrollment is registering in a vocational school. The high school I attended offered a swell opportunity that completely altered my life. During my junior and senior years of high school, I enrolled in a program called Digital Design at the vocational school. This course suited my interests in animation and video production. Aside from giving me the chance to move out of the high school, where I never seemed to fit in, the vocational school helped prepare me for higher education. While still in high school, I garnered knowledge in a variety of software programs. I even impressed my college animation professor, who allowed me to register in the more advanced courses as a sophomore.

If a traditional classroom school setting is not for you, I recommend looking into a vocational school. If you are interested in a specific area of study, this might be a viable option. Before choosing this route, however, you need to ask yourself what career you want to pursue. Some career-oriented programs offer a scholarship for a community college or a university. The vocational school I attended offered a $3,000 scholarship to a community college.

Here's another point to consider: vocational schools often have general education classes to offer. You can be enrolled full-time and not have to go back to your high school. In addition, vocational schools tend to have a very different atmosphere from that of a traditional high school. At the one I attended, there were no jocks or a "popular crowd." Rarely did bullying take place. Most of the students there were interested in a career.

If your high school does have a technical course available, you may want to check it out. Many high schools are starting to embrace the option to offer design and tech classes for students who want to pursue such careers. And science, technology, engineering, and mathematics (STEM) education courses are becoming implemented in the classrooms, offering young people who enjoy building things some enriching course options. Definitely take advantage of such opportunities if they pique your interest. If your school does not offer specialized courses that interest you, talk with your guidance counselor or a trusted teacher about alternatives.

A Quick Note to Parents

There is a new movement that has increased in scope across the United States called the Maker Movement. This movement reaches out to young people who enjoy making things, combining art, computers, science and engineering into one academic path. Many states hold events called Maker Fairs, during which people show off the items or technological feats they have built or accomplished. If your autism-related child enjoys building things, see if there is a Maker's Fair happening near your hometown. By the way, the Maker Fairs are not only for children and teens; they are open to all ages. Your whole family may enjoy it!

Which College Should You Enroll In?

This is the sixty-four-thousand-dollar question (I hope you get my reference). Before you pick a college, what will your major area of study be?

If you are undecided about your major, consider looking into a nearby community college that offers liberal arts courses. Trying this out will give you a feel for what higher education is like in terms of teachers, coursework, and routine. This presents a simpler step to take than jumping into a large university campus. If you plan on transferring to a different college, make sure your courses are accredited. I will go into more detail about transferring course credits in a later chapter.

Community colleges are also a good choice if you only want a technical or a two-year degree. They are often less expensive, and as a student, you get a lot more hands-on experience there. Community colleges are smaller and less crowded than big college campuses. As a person with Asperger's, this setting was perfect for me. The program I enrolled in had few faculty members, and the classes were small. I also received more individualized attention than I would have in a four-year program. If you have difficulty dealing with large crowds, starting out at a smaller campus might help you ease into college life.

Another option is technical schools, which provide very hands-on education and effectively prepare students for the field. However, there are some caveats. Technical schools can be very expensive and may not be fully accredited. Non-accredited schools may present costly transitions to a university.

In my senior year of high school, I visited a technical school with my father. While the campus was small and at a convenient driving distance from home, the price extended over $20,000 a year. No scholarships were offered.

If you only want a two-year degree before you move into a career in the technical field, you might want to consider either a technical school or a community college. For me, selecting an accredited two-year program that offered a transition from an associate to a bachelor's program worked best. This approach saved me time and money. It also helped me ease into college life. The sooner you can start your research, the better. You may find that some community colleges have agreements with bigger universities, which will help down the road.

The other option is to enroll in a university. While this is a more expensive option, universities tend to offer a well-rounded education. Universities focus mainly on a concept called theory. For example, if you get an associate's degree in telecommunications, the professors will often teach about technique and technical skills on how to use a camera. In a four-year degree in this field, the teachers will explain how to use a camera or how it can be utilized to achieve emotion in the viewer. These are two different concepts altogether. Technical skills are important, but so are aesthetics for a camera operator.

Four-year colleges also stress independence and urge students to become active in their campus community. Students who share similar interests can meet up, become acquainted with one another, and potentially build future friendships or work-related connections.

When I attended the university, I was surprised to find that most students were younger than those who attended the community college. A dozen if not more fellow students I met at the two-year school were married. Some even had children. In fact, one woman I became good friends with was a grandmother.

When it comes to what you want for a career, one school will be better than another for you. For example, if you want a well-rounded education, I recommend pursuing an undergraduate degree. If you want to learn a trade and move on into the work world, then I suggest a technical school or a two-year program. Even though some employers prefer a four-year degree, your knowledge and experience are what will get you the job.

If you are not sure about which school to enroll in after high school, I recommend visiting the College Navigator website. There, you can browse different colleges. Once you have chosen one, you can research the majors that each school has to offer. This website is provided by the U.S. Department of Education and has information on every college available in the United States.

ACT and SAT; Which One to Take?

There are a few things you should think about before taking either of these college-readiness tests.

First, research the college(s) you want to apply to. Certain schools require the ACT, while others are more interested in the SAT. Some colleges might not require either test. In many cases, though, they prefer one of the college-readiness tests. Rarely do colleges and universities demand both. I would not encourage taking both tests back to back (or at all). For an Aspie, having to take one of them is stressful enough.

So, what is the difference between the ACT and the SAT? The ACT focuses on what a student has learned from the classroom, which includes basic subjects like math, reading, writing, and science. From my experience, it is difficult to say which score to aim for, since colleges often request different numbers. I remember my high school guidance counselor telling me that anything below an 18 was not advisable. "Aim for a 23" he told me. "That's the average score." In my mind, attaining a higher number is best.

On the SAT, the focus is on reading, writing, and math. The SAT concentrates on a student's aptitude level instead of what he learns from the classroom. The SAT also penalizes students for wrong answers, whereas the ACT does not. The score is based on a 0-2400 rating. According to my high school guidance counselor, a score between 1500-1800 is considered an average score. I opted for the ACT in high school. I liked the concept of taking an exam that did not penalize for wrong answers. In addition, the schools I was interested in accepted the ACT.

As a freshman, I was informed that I should take one of these college-readiness tests in the winter or late spring of my junior year. The tests are created at an eleventh grade level. If you take the ACT multiple times, the highest score counts. You need to plan several months in advance in order to sign up for a college-readiness test. To get any additional information regarding these tests, approach your school guidance counselor. Also, find out which schools near you offer college-readiness tests. Your home school may very well offer some SAT or ACT examination sessions throughout the school year.

In my experience, I had to get in contact with another school district that offered the ACT. My father became an instrumental component in organizing the date and time of my examination. Be warned, the testing times are not the most desirable. It was eight o'clock in the morning when I first took the ACT. If like me you are not a morning person, you may want to try to find a test that is offered at a different time. This could mean commuting to a different area in your community.

How Can You Prepare for the ACT?

Since the ACT measures your knowledge as a student, the best way to approach it is by solving the problems in the shortest amount of time. In my experience, the length for each topic was 45 minutes. This did not provide much of a time window for me. With Asperger's, I am the type of individual who does not like strict deadlines. I made several mistakes on the ACT that cost me points.

One, I did not prepare very well for the exam. Two, I had a "yikes" moment when I learned about the rigid time rule. With my IEP, I had always been given extended time on tests and assignments. This option was now gone. I had been pushed up against a wall, figuratively speaking.

I was so anxious during the test that I could feel my heart pound like a drum during a live rock band performance. Sweat cascaded down my face. If someone had filmed me, I would have given the impression of a nervous cartoon character, ready to blast off like a rocket into space. I became heavily fixated on each question. My thought process followed like this: *Did I read the question correctly? Is the answer hidden in the question? Could the multiple-choice answer be both A and B? Is it D, all the above? No! It's never D! It has to be B or C. Those are always the best choices, right? Right?* Caught up in my own anxiety, I did not finish the test within the time limit.

The final thing that bothered me about the ACT was the testing room environment. It was small and crowded with students. I practically had no space to stretch my back. Silence filled the room to the point that I could hear the heater kicking on and off. As an Aspie, my senses very easily go into overload. The tight spaces and annoying heater noises drew my focus away from the task at hand.

When I had concluded this horrendous experience, my father asked me, "Well, how do you think you did?"

"Fine," I said, hesitantly.

Around a month later, I received a better grade than I had anticipated. But I knew I could do better. Without delay, I decided to retake the test. I learned later from my guidance counselor that students with IEPs can get extended time on college-readiness tests. My parents and I had to fill out some paperwork. Once we sorted things out, I was able to acquire 50% extra time for each section of the exam. The catch was that the original three-hour test would be nearly five hours long. The short breaks between subjects were welcomed.

Additionally, students with IEPs or special needs were split up from the other students. The room for my second attempt of the ACT did not feel as tight or compacted. This was probably because there were not many students present. Best of all, no heater hummed to life. If you are on an IEP, definitely see to it that you get extended time and a special testing environment. Look into testing accommodations that may fit your needs.

After following through the process of applying for test modifications, I settled in for more study time. I studied from a book called *ACT for Dummies*. What I like about this book were the tips and practice questions available. It gave me an idea of what taking the ACT test would be like. Another thing that helped me prepare for the ACT was timing myself when I went through the practice questions. After all, I was going to be timed for the real test.

The practice may include answers in the back. DO NOT look at them when taking the practice test. Treat the mock-up exam as if you are actually completing the ACT. Don't be afraid to underline important parts of a question. This has saved my butt countless times. If you become confused by a question, move on to the next one. There is no rule that states you must answer all the questions in order.

When studying for the ACT, do not wait until the last week or day before the test. I recommend studying as far as a month in advance. You don't need to study for four hours every day; in fact, studying too much can actually make you forget things. This has happened to me on multiple occasions. To circumvent this problem, I only studied between 30 to 60 minutes each day for the ACT. A little bit each day helped me build a solid foundation.

Before the day of the test, make sure you get plenty of sleep. Have a hearty breakfast when you wake up. Don't stuff yourself with too much food, though; your digestive system needs to be calm, without an ounce of indigestion. Bathroom breaks are prohibited during the test. The usual tips apply, like remaining calm and relaxed. It may sound cliché or easier said than done, but a confident mind outperforms one with brewing anxiety.

The reading and writing sections on the ACT can be tricky. During the reading parts, I have found that they ask a series of questions pertaining to a text. Here's my tip: I never read the whole text. In my mind, this is only wasted time. Instead, I skipped ahead to the questions and underlined the important points of the inquiries. Then I went back and skimmed through the provided text to look for particular phrases or words that relate to the questions. When I took the ACT, the questions were very specific.

However, if reading the whole text works better for you, then systematically review the questions before reading it. Write down or underline important points that the questions ask. This technique may also work well during the writing section. The version of the ACT I took had a short story and a non-fiction sample, followed by a question in which I was supposed to answer in essay format. Working smart is more effective than working hard.

And the SAT?

Since I did not take the SAT, I cannot give you nearly as much advice pertaining to this test. However, the basic tips that I have provided for the ACT may apply. One book I suggest checking out is *The Official SAT Study Guide*. This book serves as a guide and study preparation for students. It is a very reliable book, and the fact that it is written by the College Board is a plus.

Talk to your school guidance counselor for more details. She may share some additional facts and help guide you on which college-readiness test to take. Make sure you are given extended time on the exam. Finally, remember that your final score on the SAT or ACT is not the only thing that colleges review.

Note to Parents: Modifying the SAT and ACT

Earlier I covered how college-readiness tests can be modified to suit your child's autism-related needs. As a teen with Asperger's, I had no idea modifications were possible until I had approached my high school counselor. This option's availability may vary due to many factors, including where you live, what your AS child's IEP covers, and the rules of the tests. Talk with your child's school guidance counselor about test modifications. Be warned that getting approval may take some teeth pulling; I had to wait a while before I took the ACT again. It could be months before your AS child is finally approved for testing accommodations. In part, this is why you need to have your child's exam time set several months in advance.

Now, there is a chance that the request for accommodations could be denied. In that case, you either can reapply or you may have to take the test on their terms. For more information on testing accommodations, visit the College Board website.

Another thing you can do to help your AS teenager is go over some mock-up ACT/SAT questions with him. After reviewing the math section from the ACT practice book, I approached my father for some help on the questions I had marked wrong. My father, a math wizard, sat down with me and went over some tricks and tips on how to quickly solve the problems. After revising my study experiences, I ended up scoring much higher in math on my second try at the ACT.

If your AS child is struggling with a subject, you may want to look into tutoring or after-school mentoring. The former may cost some money, but one-on-one interaction could be beneficial. Based on my experience with Asperger's, it is hard for me to learn in a group setting. Having personalized attention with a mentor might benefit your AS child.

You want to consider taking a road trip with your child to the testing location before test day. Familiarize him with the setting and building. Part of the reason why I didn't do well on my first try at the ACT was because of the environment. I remember waiting in a long line to fill out my registration form. Hundreds of students were waiting in line, crowding the tight hallways. This atmosphere freaked me out. You do not want your AS child to be even more anxious on testing day. Attention to detail regarding the test experience will ensure your child's best possible outcome.

Chapter 3

Applications & Scholarships

Applying for college is a very daunting process. Even though search engines are good research tools, they do not tell you which school to enroll in. If you find yourself seeking information about colleges, you can turn to others for advice, such as a teacher or a guidance counselor. In my final year of high school, I had a really swell Digital Design teacher who called me over to his desk one day during class.

"I know you're not interested in the community college our program is affiliated with," he told me. He was right. I did not feel comfortable driving forty miles one way to go to school. Living away from home did not appeal to me either.

He continued. "There's another community college, part of a bigger university, that might work better for you," he informed me.

He then opened the school's website on his computer, which featured a cool video filmed, directed and performed by students. The movie short was about a young man wandering in a dimly lit hallway, fighting off zombies with only a handgun and a flashlight. *They have these productions in college?* I wondered. *Sign me up!* It did not take me long to fill out an application for that school.

Your parents may also provide some guidance and school recommendations. They may also present some more practical advice for you regarding price ranges, commuting, and the possibilities of living on campus.

Transitioning to a new environment without any planning can be frightening. For people with autism, the anxiety of entering an unknown atmosphere is exponentially terrifying. As an individual with Asperger's, I am a creature of habit; change is not something I easily accept. With that said, attending the suburban community college campus of a major university proved to be an easy transition. If you desire to attend a big university in another state or country, by all means, go for it. Just prepare for daily anxieties that may arise, such as not knowing how to get around. This all falls on your shoulders.

What You Need to Complete College Applications

The actual process for college applications are not all that complicated in comparison to say finding a school that piques your interest. Each time I applied for a college, they requested my class transcript, my personal information, my college-readiness test scores, the application form I had filled out, and a written essay.

I quickly discovered that the written essays were the hardest part of any college application. The questions asked were usually self-reflective: What do you hope to achieve at our university? What career do you plan on pursuing? What are your life dreams?

While these inquiries may seem silly, this essay is one of the most important components of a college application. Your answers determine whether you are a good fit for the college and its program. That is why it is important to pick both a college and a program that fulfills your wants and needs. You need to choose a major that relates to both your strengths and interests.

When I applied for a film study degree at a state university, I emphasized my fascination with movies and knowledge of the different processes that are involved in completing one. Incorporating that type of mindset is what makes a great college application essay. Although I cannot tell you what to write (only you can decide that), I can urge you not to take shortcuts on this step. Give your essay some time and thought.

I recommend that you type your essay in a Word document and read it out loud to catch any structural problems. Have your parents take a look at it to make sure you express yourself in a positive and direct manner. I know what it is like to write something that reads really great in your mind, but when read out loud, it sounds atrocious.

The college application may prompt you to write the essay by hand on a sheet of paper or on the application itself. In either case, I always created a Word document to gather my thoughts first. Once I typed the essay and read it to a family member, I then transcribed it by hand. Though using this method may take some extra time, it will make your essay much cleaner and stronger.

How to Find and Get Scholarships

The search for scholarships is just as strenuous as finding a college. Applying for a scholarship is never a guarantee you'll get it. I have requested at least a dozen of them over the years as a college student and I only obtained a couple of them. I have learned that most scholarships usually only apply to a specific school. For instance, when I received a $3,000 scholarship for a community college, it only worked for that school.

More often than not, you need to contact the college to obtain a list of scholarships you can apply for. This way you will find out directly what grants or scholarships the college has available for students. You can acquire scholarship applications at the college's admissions office.

Going online and signing up for a website that offers scholarships may not be a bad idea, but I would not totally rely on such services. Also, be careful; never sign up for a service that charges money. Most likely it is a scam, especially if it asks for a credit card number. You should be suspicious of any website that asks for money. Also be cautious when providing personal information that could put you on mailing lists that you want no part of.

When choosing a scholarship, only submit an application for ones that are relevant to you. Remember that what you do in high school does affect your college experience. I had a very high GPA in high school. Because of that, I qualified for an academic scholarship for my freshman year in college. However, I had to maintain at least a 3.5 GPA to keep the scholarship.

This may seem hard to believe, but some scholarships are awarded based on race and ethnicity. If you fall under the non-white or minority category, you could qualify for scholarships to help fund your education. For more information on these prospects, do some research.

You can always apply for more than one scholarship, but from my experience, it is hard to obtain two or more. During my sophomore year of college, I applied for five different scholarships and did not receive a single one. That is why it is important to sign up for as many as you can. There is never a guarantee.

Applying for a scholarship is very similar to filling out a college application form. Once you have the scholarship application, you need to list your information, add your school transcript, and write an essay. When writing your scholarship essay, explain why you are the ideal candidate. Emphasize what the scholarship will achieve for you as a student. For instance, explain how it will help you on your journey as a college student and share a few details about yourself.

The Last Run for Applications

Both scholarship and college applications can be either submitted online or mailed to the school. This depends on the school's requirements. I found that the hardest part of submitting applications is the waiting period. It can take anywhere from a few weeks to several months before you hear a response. This can be very trying as your anxiety builds. Did they reject my application? Did they even receive it?

This is all part of the waiting game. The best thing you can do is not worry about it. I know that sounds absurd, especially for us Aspies who can't let things go. But frankly, there is no point in fretting over circumstances beyond your control. Instead, focus your attention elsewhere; do your day-to-day activities and retain those as your areas of concentration.

I recommend waiting at least a month before following up with the college about your application for admission. Often you will receive a notification in the mail (most schools are old-fashioned that way) on whether you have been accepted or not. It might be soul crushing when you find out that you haven't been accepted, but never take it as an insult if you get rejected. Colleges, specifically large universities, are very selective of which students they welcome into their campus. That is why you should apply to several colleges. "Never put all your eggs in one basket," as my mother used to tell me.

Notes to Parents: What Can You Do to Help?

College hunting and preparation is very difficult. Your AS child will need a lot of help from you to make this transition. During this part of your teenager's life, there are several things you can do to help.

Organizing and Proofreading the Applications. I remember the tedious processes involved with filling out college and scholarship applications. All the boxes and lines on these applications can be confusing and sometimes intimidating for your AS child. Take some time to do a final look-over your AS child's application. We all make mistakes, so a second pair of eyes never hurts. My parents reviewed my applications to make sure I didn't miss any of the check boxes or tiny, underlined sections.

Another thing you may want to consider is sitting in on your AS child's college research. Sometimes college websites can be perplexing. Links can be challenging to find. Sometimes you have to dig deep before you can acquire an email address or even a phone number to contact the college office. Fortunately, most websites are not hard to navigate.

Road Trip and School Tours. Most colleges have campus tours that can be informative and fun, while also generalized and informal. Students of the college are most often the tour guides. The reason behind these tours is to both showcase the school's facilities and to catch your teenager's attention regarding the campus' activities.

College programs also hold seminars for students and parents alike. Most of the time, the department head will stress the advantages and successes the program has to offer. While this is all fine and dandy, the seminar does not often give much detail on classrooms, projects, and teachers, and these are the more important factors you and your AS child need to know.

To prepare your AS teenager for higher education, I strongly recommend you contact the school your child is interested in and take a personal field trip there. During my senior year I visited a university, a community college, and a technical school. These three trips helped formulate in my mind what type of environment, structure, and atmosphere the institutions had available. Such components are vital for people with autism-related disorders. The school environment and structure is as important as the program curriculum and school staff. Experiencing the school environment firsthand will provide you an opportunity to experience the school's atmosphere.

Taking these individualized tours also gives your teenager a chance to see what the teachers, classrooms, and projects are like. This type of visit is like a movie trailer, which gives you a chance to decide whether you would like to see the movie, or in this case, apply to the school. If you contact the college office in advance and set up an appointment, you can have a more formal tour as well as discuss options with one of the institution's faculty members.

When my father and I visited a community college, I met with the department's secretary and spoke one-on-one with a student who was working on his capstone project. This little journey showed me what to anticipate from the program. I cannot stress how important it is for you to do this with your AS teenager. It will significantly help her adjust to the new school environment.

Looking back, going from a vocational school to a two-year program and then from there to a university environment allowed me to adjust in smaller steps. This option might be worth considering for your child. Going from high school to a huge university could be too much of a transition. Studying, adjusting to different teaching styles, and knowing where classes are located is more than enough to put on your AS child's plate.

Note to Parents: Disability Services

When your AS child is researching colleges, make sure the school has a service for people with disabilities. This should not be an issue, since many colleges and universities have such programs available. When making a college visit with your child, I recommend organizing an appointment with a representative of the school's disability services department. Doing this will help gauge what the program has to offer and how it operates. Knowing how the disability service's department helps students can play a determining factor in whether the school is a good fit for your AS child. Ask about the testing facilities, the different accommodations the service has to offer, and the guidelines they require from teachers. The type of modifications they have may vary.

After your AS child is accepted into a school, you will need to get in contact with the school's disability service program. Expect that there will be some documents and forms that need to be filled out either by you or your child. The most important thing they will need is a copy of your AS child's IEP. Sending that over, along with the requested information, will help smooth the transition. It will take some time, probably a few weeks, because all of your child's data needs to enter the school's system. After about three weeks, give them a call to find out if they have received your child's information and if it has been processed.

Colleges are open year-round, except for weekends and most holidays. Making a simple phone call, preferably in the late morning or early afternoon, should suffice. From personal experience, calling after 4:00 PM can result in a voicemail loop, and your message might be missed or accidentally erased.

Chapter 4

Entering College

The first year of college can be downright scary. Most if not all of your friends from high school will not be there with you. You will be surrounded with new faces in a new environment, and you might not know what to expect from anyone in this new setting. Colleges also hold many different requirements for incoming freshmen. These unknown factors can make you feel like a fish out of water. As difficult as it sounds, try not to become overwhelmed by all these experiences. I have many tips to offer that I hope will make your college journey less frightening.

How to Minimize Costs

The cost of a college education can strain or exceed your family's resources.

Tuition is not the only cost you'll face; there are program fees, campus life fees, parking fees, traveling costs, food, books, computers, other technology items, and class supplies. Most scholarships do not cover all of the costs you'll face. If the remaining costs are overwhelming, financial aid is there to assist. Colleges have staff members available to help students in this area.

One of the best ways to save money in college is by working with your academic advisor. This person will help guide you to decide which classes you need to take in order to graduate. It is imperative to take only courses that are required for your major. Do not get sidetracked and register for classes that seem interesting. I made this mistake during my second year of college. Instead of signing up for the core class I needed to take, I enrolled in a free elective. As a result, I had to wait another school year to graduate, since the last course I needed was only offered during the fall term.

You may find that some core classes are only offered in one semester. Schedule an appointment as soon as possible with your academic advisor before registering for the next semester. An academic advisor may be assigned to you, make sure to utilize this resource. He may have a worksheet that lists all the core classes available by semester. Follow this document and plan your courses in advance.

College classes are grouped in levels, like they were in high school. For instance, a course at a 100 level may be a freshman class, and the 400 level might be a senior course. Once you are beyond the entry-level classes, you will face your prerequisite classes. You must complete these before you can register for the higher-level classes.

I found this system confusing at first. There were so many options and tons of information to keep straight. I learned that meeting

with my academic advisor throughout my first year was very beneficial. My experiences during my freshman year taught me a bit about
how to navigate the class registration system.

If you can't get into a required class, there are a couple of things
you can try. One, you can petition the teacher to get into the class.
Two, you can check to see if there is another course you can take to
match the credit for that class. Three, you can settle for taking the
class on another day or at a different time.

Because I registered for classes at the earliest possible date,
I did not become anxious about getting into the classes I wanted. Many required classes fill up quickly, so build your next class
schedule early.

Email and Student IDs

Once I registered for college, there were two important things I needed to do. First, I had to obtain my student ID. I simply had to walk
down to school security and visit one of the guards. Going to security may sound a bit intimidating, but it was not at all that bad. I
informed the guard that I was a new student. He asked me for my
driver's license and handed me some forms to fill out (just what I
needed, another case of college bureaucracy!). After completing the
forms, he took my mug shots—I mean, uh, my ID photo. He then
printed the ID with my name and photo. In other words, it was just
like going to the DMV.

Second, I needed a school email account. This was simple to acquire as well. All I had to do was visit the school's IT department.

Finally, no forms! Be prepared to learn the ins and outs of the college online network.

Enrolling in Classes

Registering for courses should be an easy process. Your college may have an educational site that you can use to sign up for classes. The college I attended offered a website for students to sign up for their courses.

There are some things you should think about when organizing your course schedule. First, check to see what time classes are being offered. If you are taking a class that is on Mondays and Wednesdays from 8:00 AM to 9:30 AM and you need to take a core class that is at the exact same time, you must make a sacrifice. It is best to enroll in the courses for your major first before registering in any other class.

Some liberal arts courses will most likely be required for your major. They are usually offered year-round at different, more flexible times. Classes within a specific major are rigid. Your major is the top priority.

You may very well have to juggle the class sections to make a workable schedule. I recommend taking as many classes as you can within the least amount of days. For my first semester of college, I was on campus for only three days of the week. As a result, my Thursday schedule went from 9:00 AM to 9:30 PM. Though the hours sucked, I had two days off for study time. Cramming a ton of classes in the same day may seem like a hefty load, but it has a great payoff for both study and free time.

This option does not always work out. At the community college I attended, classes met once a week for three hours. In comparison, the university I attended had classes that met two times a week for an hour and a half. Therefore, I spent a lot more time at the university campus versus at the community college.

The amount of hours you take per semester is entirely up to you. Just know that a full-time student takes 12 or more credit hours for each semester. Some say that, for every hour you spend in a class, you need to put forth an additional one to three hours a week. For the minimum full-time course load, you could be putting in around 50 hours of class and study. Being a full-time college student is equivalent to a full-time job.

If you want to save money, consider taking between 14 to 18 credit hours per semester. This may be tough, especially in your freshman year. In my first semester at college, I tried to take 15 credit hours, and I lasted two weeks before I dropped a class. I learned to take a course load that I could handle; twelve hours were plenty for me.

Disability Services

Disability services will be one of your most vital lifelines. During my first day in college, I discovered that my accommodations depended solely on me. After filling out some forms, I was told that I had to get all of my teacher's signatures on my accommodations form. For the remainder of my first day in college, I approached all my professors and requested their signatures. Once I had returned the form to disability services, I was set for the rest of the semester. I had to do this for every single term until I graduated.

This process may be different for each school, but in most cases, your accommodations are your responsibility. No one will approach a teacher for you and request extended time for a test. You have to advocate for yourself. With my Asperger's, I find it awkward to approach people that I don't know, and I had to overcome this challenge to get my teachers' signatures.

Professors usually have no problem signing forms, but you may have to remind them of your accommodations. To resolve this issue, I made a copy of my accommodations form for each professor.

I recommend using disability services when it comes to taking tests. In my experience, I was given a quiet environment to take my tests in. This accommodation only worked if I had organized an appointment three days in advance. It was important for me to know the date and time of each exam. I could not simply walk in and take my test. Disability services have rules.

You don't always have to use disability services for your tests; taking them in class is an option. This could be advantageous, particularly if you are confused by a question. There have been times where I got flustered over how a test question was worded. Raising my hand and asking the teacher for clarification proved helpful. At disability services though, there is no one there to help you. You may get extra time, but you are on your own.

Books, Books, Books

Many of my former professors had required textbooks that were thick, lengthy, and pricy. Initially, I purchased my books at the school bookstore. I found there were plenty of advantages to this approach.

One, I could easily access the required textbook. As an Aspie, I found that getting my books sooner rather than later helped me quell my anxiety. There were times when a book was sold out, and this was never to my liking. Usually, however, it only took about a week before new stock came in. I could count on the bookstore.

A second reason I liked going to the school bookstore was because it gave students a chance to either rent or purchase used books. I always opted for the latter. I learned from my college that renting a book came with a time limit. A student could only hold onto it for part of the semester before renewing it, and this came with an extra cost. In buying used books, I found that most of the copies were in fairly decent shape. I would strongly consider this option when acquiring your textbooks. Sometimes you might have to buy a new book. For several of my liberal arts classes, I had to get the latest edition. These books often included an activation code for online assignments.

In other situations, you might be required to purchase a book outside of the school. I had one teacher who assigned the class an old book that was only available on Amazon. Worse still, she did not tell us about it until the first day of class. The first reading assignment was due the following week. This was very frustrating. I had to scramble to order a book and receive it in time to complete my assignment.

However, this experience has shown me that I could purchase textbooks outside of the school bookstore. On some occasions, I found required textbooks cheaper online than at the bookstore. This could be an option worth considering.

Additional Accessories

The colleges I attended were pretty old-fashioned when it came to assignments and tests. I always needed a #2 pencil and a notebook. On the flip side, some of my professors allowed laptops in their classes. If you own a laptop, ask your professor if you may bring it to class for note-taking purposes.

As a student, I quickly learned that a laptop could be a real lifesaver for in-class note-taking. Writing by hand slows me down. During the time I write one important detail, I miss the next one. Using a laptop also helped me retain in-class lectures. You will be doing a lot more writing in college than in high school. A computer can be quite beneficial if you have terrible handwriting (like me). Some major programs do require laptops.

As an individual with Asperger's, I crave structure and organization. For each semester, I bought a binder for each class. This helped me manage all my class papers. Back in my high school days, I always used color-coded folders to arrange what assignments and papers belonged to which class. Although this worked on a term-by-term basis for general education, it was not so useful in college.

I learned that professors, particularly for liberal arts classes, load you up with course documents. Binders are so much sturdier than folders. If you accidentally drop a binder, it will not fall apart like a papered folder. For each three-ring binder, I labeled the front with the course name. I went the extra mile by purchasing dividers, naming them as follows:

- Notes
- In-Class Assignments
- Homework
- Study Guides
- Tests/Quizzes

As the semester progressed, I set one day a week to put all my papers together in the right binders and dividers. Writing down dates on my class documents was essential for the success of this process, and I arranged them in order from old to new. Keeping a system like this will make college a much more organized and somewhat less stressful experience for you. You never have to worry about misplacing papers. It may sound like a lot of work, but it has a huge payoff.

Projects and Assignments

Most of your grades in college will be based on exams and big projects (papers, essays, presentations). If you are a fine arts major, you will probably spend most of your time making visual or audio-related assignments. These are cumbersome in nature and require an equal amount of creativity and commitment. I discovered in college that teachers rarely assigned group projects; that came later in higher-level courses.

If you are in a program or major that requires using software or equipment, I recommend using the school's facilities. When I was getting my associate's degree, several core classes I had to take involved video production. Being an Aspie, it was hard for me to wrap my head around the concept of sharing and working with others. I always preferred to work with my own gear. I was tempted to get my own camera. My mother told me up front that neither she nor my dad would buy me a video camera. At first I was disheartened. *Great, how am I supposed to complete my assignments now?* I then realized that spending a lot of money on a camera that I might use for only a couple of classes was ridiculous. So, I trained myself to use the school's equipment. I found the equipment managers to be very helpful.

Be extra careful with the school's gear. Many colleges have a policy that if you break something, you buy it. The rules might be different at your college. The school I went to was not overly fond of students who did not return the equipment within a 24-hour window. Failure to turn the gear in on time led to penalties. I was on a clock like Jack Bauer. Being on the equipment manager's good side proved crucial for me. In some instances, you may have to purchase or rent equipment from a retailer. If this is the case, talk with the school faculty on what items you need for the program or class.

In addition, colleges offer computer labs for students. If money is tight, you may want to complete your assignments at such facilities.

The catch is that you can only work in these labs during the assigned days and hours. Check to see if the facilities are open on Saturdays.

During my sophomore year, I made extra trips to school on weekends in order to use a computer program to complete required assignments. If you work on a school computer, make sure you have a copy of your files with you; do not leave them on the school's computer. I made this mistake once. As a result, I could not access my file until the following school week. Thankfully, another user had not deleted the file. To prevent this problem from happening again, I always carried a thumb drive to copy my files over. Keeping track of your stuff is critical.

The Syllabus, Daily Planner, and the Highlighter

The syllabus, or "silly bus," as one of my funny college professors called it, is the text that outlines what topics the class covers, what students will learn, and most importantly, when assignments are due. You will be given a copy of the syllabus at the start of every class. DO NOT lose this document. I always hole punched and placed my syllabus at the front of my binder. Every time I opened my course binder, I knew when my assignments were due.

There are two other items that made college go smoother for me. One was a daily planner. I used this to write down the assignments I needed to complete on a weekly basis. I always found these planners at the school bookstore. At just a few dollars, the investment was well worth it. The other item I always had with me was a highlighter. As an Aspie college student, I never knew when I might need to highlight some important information from a book or to set myself a reminder for a crucial project. These three items will help make your college experience go a lot more smoothly. Get yourself into a habit of organizing important documents and writing down vital assignments.

First Notes to Parents: Laying Down Some Ground Rules

For my college education, I made a two-part deal with my parents. First, I would pursue a college degree. Second, they would cover all costs up to an undergraduate degree, as long as I finished and did not take any time off. I fulfilled both parts of the bargain and came out with an associate's and a bachelor's degree.

How your AS child decides to finish his education is up to him. However, you need to instill in him the notion that he must either complete his degree or drop out permanently. A college degree is an all-or-nothing deal, there is no middle ground. This is why it is important for your AS child to find a degree that fits his interests. Otherwise, he may not succeed.

Second Note to Parents: Handling Bills

Tuition can be paid in three different ways. The first and most old-fashioned method is writing out a check and delivering it to the college registrar's office. For every semester in college, my mom wrote the check, and I delivered it. The only problem was waiting in the long lines. Paying the school bill earlier rather than later minimized this issue.

The second method is paying online. Many colleges and universities offer a service on their websites for students to pay their bills, on which they simply log in and use their credit card. There is a caveat with this approach. Depending on the cost of the school's tuition, it could push you beyond your monthly credit card plan.

Another catch that may arise from paying tuition bills online is the additional fees involved. The student has to spend a little extra money in order to pay tuition in this manner. If you want to be frugal, I would disregard this method entirely.

The final way of paying tuition is by mailing the check to the college registrar's office. The concern with this approach is the uncertainty of whether the office received the envelope. It is very easy for mail to fall through the cracks, particularly at a large university. It is unlikely that you will obtain a receipt. If you select this approach, I recommend buying a certificate of mailing for the sent envelope. This proves that you had mailed the check from the post office to the college. In addition, I strongly advise requesting a return receipt to verify the paid bill.

Third Note to Parents: Give Your AS Child Some Space

I grew up with helicopter parents. They helped me with just about everything in school—folders, homework, assignments, teachers, you name it. The college transition made this approach somewhat difficult for my parents. They could no longer guide me like they did during my high school years. Their powers were now limited. All responsibility for assignments and projects fell solely on me. There were times where I became frustrated with both homework and teachers alike, yet I managed to find ways to solve any college-related issue.

Because parental control is limited, college is a time for your AS child to grow into his own person. While I needed the extra help in the transitioning phase, I carried my weight as time went on. Your AS child will be exposed to many different things in college. This is greatly expanded if she is heading off to a large campus. I cannot tell you how your AS teen may respond to such a new environment, so it is up to you to adapt to what may come.

In my early childhood years, I exhibited what doctors called severe autism. One psychologist told my mother that I would never be able to drive, go to college, or live on my own. As a young adult now, I have far exceeded this doctor's expectations. Your AS child could mature and surpass his early clinical predictions.

It takes baby steps for Aspies to progress in life. The freshman year of college is like an Eskimo paddling on a chunk of ice into the ocean. College is all about self-reliance and guidance; you either paddle or sink. If your AS child feels ready for college, support her. Do not force her into attending college if she is not ready—this can backfire terribly. She could have a meltdown within the first couple of weeks.

For the first week of my freshman year, my classes loaded me up with 10 chapters of reading and three writing assignments. All were due the following week. I almost walked up to the college office for a collection of withdrawal slips. However, I survived because I studied every day and communicated with my parents when I needed help.

College is hardcore. Some teachers intimidate their students by loading them up with homework for the first couple of weeks. The students who are serious about their education persevere, whereas the others end up dropping classes. Be there for your AS teen. Listen when she needs to talk.

There could be times where your AS child will not want to share her thoughts. Unfortunately, there is nothing you can do during such times. Like most other people, we Aspies clam up and sometimes feel the need to resolve our problems alone. It was not until my college years when I realized that no person could be his own island. We have to rely on others to succeed. Even though this may sound corny, I strongly advise that you highlight the importance of relying on other people with your child. College teaches students many features of life, and among them is the significance of teamwork.

Chapter 5

College Transfers & Changing Majors

ransferring classes and college credit deserves its own little chapter, because these processes are very challenging and often time consuming. For you college-aged Aspie readers who plan on transitioning from one school to another, read this chapter carefully.

Transferring Credits: From High School to College

It is possible to transfer classes from high school for college credit. One option is to enroll in Advanced Placement (AP) classes. Your grade and completion of these courses can count towards liberal arts classes like English, math, and history. How many hours you get depends on the college.

Some universities offer Internet-based classes for high school seniors. However, these classes may only count for credit at a specific school. This is certainly something to look into if you have been accepted to a college.

You may want to check to see if your high school allows students to enroll in college classes. Approach your guidance counselor with this idea. Before you consider this option though, decide if you can handle the workload. Going this route means completing both high school and college homework at the same time. Like with online college classes, the credits may only apply to that specific college.

Later in my college experience, I learned that students could test out of entry-level classes. Had I taken foreign language in high school, this may have helped me fulfill that requirement in college.

Transferring Credits: From College to College

Before you choose to extend your education, think very carefully about what degree you want to pursue next. During my final year at the community college, I had to decide whether I should further my education or not. After pondering on several paths, I applied to the art school. There were many steps I had to take in order to successfully transfer into the new college. It felt like starting my education over, but I had a couple of years of college behind me.

I had to fill out a transfer application and send over my college transcript to the school's admissions office. An essay was also required. Once I had done these things, there was the waiting period. It was about a month before I received acceptance into the college. From experience, transferring into a different college within the same university was not all that difficult.

Transferring from one university to another, though, could be a whole different matter. I cannot tell you what to anticipate. The most important thing you need to find out is which of your classes will transfer into the new school. Liberal arts courses may not be a problem, but advanced courses that relate to your major may not make the cut. In my case, the university had an articulation agreement.

This agreement listed the classes from my two-year program that would transfer into the four-year program. I learned from this agreement that not all of my classes would transfer. I had accumulated over 100 hours of classes at the community college, but only 60 hours applied toward my undergraduate degree. The other 40 hours counted but only as free electives. Colleges usually require for students to enroll in a couple of free electives. Do not go overboard with them like I did!

Transitioning to a new school that does not have an articulation agreement can be problematic. While wrapping up my associate's, one of the schools I looked into had a design program whose five-year curriculum had no agreements with any college. If I had enrolled in that program, I would have started as a freshman. For that reason, I did not register for that school. Consider these policies when transferring to another college.

Changing Majors

After being enrolled in the art school for two weeks, I realized I had picked the wrong college. The only classes I enjoyed were the drawing courses. I knew deep down that I would grow bored with observational drawing. Worse, no animation or 3D courses were offered in the program, much less the school. In fact, the college was so outdated that the faculty still taught the old-school methods of photography. In the back of my mind, I could not help but wonder how a Daguerreotype would help me land a career.

The fact that some of my teachers were a bit crazy assisted in my final decision to transfer out of the school. For one class, a professor had an assignment called "Marie Antoinette lying on the floor." We were left to determine what that meant. Many students, like me, did not know what to do. Being an Aspie, I did not understand how Marie Antoinette lying on the floor could be a project.

The teacher expected his students to work on the project without question. Most of the time, I sat in the room, waiting for the class to end. I find myself uncomfortable in unstructured environments.

When I got a chance to share an idea with the teacher, he shot it down. He either did not like where my thoughts went or found a flaw in the concept. Looking back now, I know he was just playing the devil's advocate, but at the time, I could not help but think of him as uncaring and somewhat mean-spirited.

I quickly realized that this course, much less the program, was not for me. I dropped the course and focused my energies on the drawing classes. I ended up transferring into a program that was an extension of what I had studied at the community college. The new school had an atmosphere I felt more comfortable with, and it explored topics that were more to my liking. My brief stay at the art school taught me that sometimes you have to experience something in order to realize it is not for you.

There will be aspects in college that could push you out of your comfort zone. Higher education intends to prepare students for the work world, which means adding stress like deadlines for projects. However, a program or an environment that constantly makes you feel out of your element is not worth enduring.

Changing majors, especially mid-year, can be very troublesome. First you can withdraw from the most challenging courses of your previous major. When I dropped that oddball class with the Marie Antoinette project, I felt a huge wave of relief. You may want to try and enroll in classes that will count toward your new major. If you are too far into the semester to switch classes, then you are stuck with your current courses for the remainder of the semester. At the start of the next semester, you'll have a fresh start.

You could drop all of your classes, but you risk losing your scholarship and any financial aid you have. It will also become much harder to enroll in a new program. I ran into this scenario with the art school. I had received a $4,200 scholarship, which covered the next two years of my schooling. If I had left the art school, I would have lost the scholarship. Colleges can be finicky that way. Think out all of your options before making any big decisions. Speak with your academic advisor; she will help you with your next course of action. If the classes become difficult, never be afraid to seek help from your parents. They know you best.

There is the frightening possibility that you may not get accepted into the new program. In that case, continue to go to college, but list yourself as an undecided major. I suggest taking liberal arts classes. From my experience, these types of classes are less demanding and have a more traditional classroom setting. Being in an undecided major can give you a chance to explore intro-level classes of different programs, which may help you get a better feel for your educational interests. The hours you accumulate will apply toward your graduation requirements. Furthermore, you will maintain scholarship eligibility if you continue as a full-time student.

However, do not be an undecided major for too long. Being a student for four years does not guarantee graduation. You also do not want to jump from one school to the next only to drop out again; this will get you nowhere.

Apply for a program that interests you. Be prepared to have a backup plan. If you are not accepted into your first choice, apply to your secondary one. Never limit yourself to just one possibility. As an Aspie, I really loved video production, but I also loved writing. I pursued a program in the electronic media program, with the plan that, if that did not pan out, I would pursue journalism.

Remain Calm

I panicked when I discovered that the art school was not for me. I made one frantic phone call after another to my parents. "This place is not for me," "The teachers don't make sense," and the ever-popular "This school is loony" became my new catchphrases for the whole semester.

The people at the art school were alien to me in terms of personality and sometimes in appearance. I coped with this uncomfortable environment by listening to familiar music. Putting in the ear buds and tuning everything out had a unique way of resetting my mind.

I also distanced myself from the classroom. Sitting further away and observing the class made my experience less intense. Bathroom and drinking fountain breaks gave me opportunities to walk away and settle my anxious mind and avoid my Aspie meltdowns.

A little coping mechanism that helped me through my high school days was carrying a stress ball. Small and convenient, I could pull the ball out and squeeze it whenever I felt tense. There is some sort of connection between squeezing soft things and releasing stress. I don't know the science or psychology behind it, but it has worked for me. Now, reflecting upon that time in college, I wish had taken my stress ball with me.

Getting accepted into the eMedia program lifted a big weight from my chest. I felt like I had been rescued from Mars. As hard as such a situation is, the best thing you can do is endure. Sticking with the program will show you what the college workload and atmosphere is like. Even if you despise it, you may still learn a thing or two in the classroom. Do not slip on attendance or intentionally bomb classes. Getting an F in class is a permanent grade in college. This will kill your chances of any future scholarships.

Note to Parents: Be an Advisor

My parents suggested that I pursue a bachelor's degree. When I was wrapping up the two-year program, I needed to decide where to continue my education. The program at the community college had an articulation agreement for two four-year colleges. I had to decide which one would be a better fit for me. We talked quite a bit, weighing out my options, and we decided on the art school, which ended up being the wrong choice.

While talking things over with your AS child is important, you need to think about his strengths and style of learning. In my experience, the art school had too much of a think-outside-the-box learning environment. There was no structure. Attending that school showed me that sometimes the only way to know if a college is a right fit is by attending it. Visiting the college with your child and learning as much as you can about the school's atmosphere would also be a huge benefit.

You must intervene if your AS child finds herself hopping from major to major. It is very easy to get sidetracked. I know, because I have 40 hours of free electives to prove it!

Some time away from the classroom could also be helpful. If your AS child feels the need to take a semester off to get her mind straight, this might be an option worth pursuing. I recommend this only as a last resort and under extreme circumstances. Keep in mind that, once she leaves the school, getting back in may present an additional challenge.

Chapter 6

Teachers

The overall atmosphere in college is quite different from what I faced in high school. I found that higher education embraces individuality, diversity, and above all open-mindedness.

On my first day at college, one of the professors outlined the requirements for his class in a rather long-winded speech during which he informed us that once we entered his class, we were considered professionals. College is the first step in your career. What you do from there determines your future.

The Basic Overview of College Teachers

Most college teachers want you to succeed. However, they won't coddle or force you to complete your assignments. Self-reliance is expected of college students. If you fall behind on assignments or miss a day of class, it is your responsibility to catch up. Your teacher will not update you on missed class material. Whenever I asked a teacher about a missed class assignment, I got one of two answers: either check the syllabus or ask a classmate.

As an Aspie, this approach was a bit of a shock. In high school, I had special needs teachers who helped me along. In college, even though I had disability services helping me, they did not provide the same level of assistance as I had previously received. However, they provided me a note-taker who was a student in my class, and I received their notes through the school website. I had this assistance for my first year in college. In my third year though, I was able to return this favor to other students in need (and, by the way, I got paid).

I have found there are three types of teachers in college. The first kind are rare; these are the ones who should not be teaching. Such individuals exhibit undesirable attributes like arriving late for class, frequently being in a bitter mood, and not meeting with students for office hours. Other unpleasant characteristics may include unfair grading, disorganization, favoritism, and verbal abusive. I encountered such teachers among the tenured faculty. The stereotype of the old cranky, professor does exist in rare cases.

The second kind are the great professors who are generally enthusiastic and love to teach. These individuals are often willing to set time aside and work one on one with their students. They grade fairly and give honest feedback. I consider these individuals to be real mentors. In fact, a couple of my teachers provided reference letters for me when I was looking for a job. I have been very fortunate to find such wonderful people.

Lastly, the third group is composed of the majority of teachers. They are generally fair, easy going, and talented instructors, but they are not individuals who will inspire you.

What Else Do You Need to Know About College Professors?

From my experience, college professors don't always hold their students to a high standard. For instance, if you walk in late to class, it is not likely that will you be ridiculed or penalized for your grade. However, this is not always the case. In my capstone course during the two-year program, the head professor singled out a student for showing up late. The teachers in this program included attendance as part of the grade.

The two-year school I went to had a three-strike attendance policy. If a student had three or more unexcused absences, his grade dropped a whole letter. This policy provided another reason for me to be present in class. Your school may not have this rule.

Being an Aspie, I am very disciplined about attendance, promptness, and preparedness. I always arrived a few minutes early to each class and finished my assignments a couple of days ahead of time. For this program, classes met once a week for three hours. I had six days to complete my projects, which were very extensive. I read my chapters and met with the equipment manager in case I needed to check out gear. Try your best not to fall behind. College moves way too fast for you to ever catch up if you do.

One of the most important things you can do is show respect to the teacher. That means paying attention to her lectures, turning off your cell phone, and raising your hand when you have a question. On the first day of class, I always asked my teachers if I could use my laptop for note-taking purposes. Most were fine with this. There were a couple who said no.

Unless you have a form from disability services that allows you to have a laptop or a student note-taker, honor the professor's wishes. You do not want to start off the semester by antagonizing your professors. Some teachers may not even care how you take notes, but in my experience, the professors at the community college were more sensitive about this matter than the ones at the four-year school. It also depends on the teacher.

There is the possibility that your teacher may end up modifying the due dates of assignments in the syllabus. For one semester in my senior year, the university closed down for seven days due to inclement weather. My German II class modified the syllabus three times during the course of the term. Being an Aspie, this frustrated me quite a bit. I had to continually print out a new syllabus and toss out the previous one.

If you are going to miss a day of class, contact your professor either by phone or email. As a person with Asperger's, communicating with others is very difficult for me. With my college email though, I could very easily send messages to my professor. I did not have to ask my questions or express my concerns in the classroom setting. Inadvertently, I discovered that teachers were very appreciative when I notified them of an upcoming absence. Showing a little common courtesy goes a long way.

Teachers and Assignments

As an Aspie, I tend to obsess over things such as class assignments. I have to finish them on time, preferably a couple of days early. If the course seems like a lot of work (which most are), focus more study time on items like projects and exams, as opposed to quizzes. It is logical to ace a final that is worth 30% of your grade versus a quiz that is only 1%. I made the mistake of focusing too much attention on inconsequential elements of the course during a freshman photography class. With my AS, I have to do well on all of my assignments, even small ones. I spent hours studying for the weekly quizzes and only a half hour on my assignments. While I did well on the quizzes, I did poorly on the projects. I quickly had to readjust my homework strategy.

Do not complete your assignments haphazardly. Teachers in college will not accept late work. As one of my teachers said, "If you turn in an assignment late, you get a big goose egg" (meaning a zero). If a professor does accept late work (which is rare), it comes at a consequence, like a letter grade lower. In such a case, handing in a late assignment is better than not turning it in.

If you find yourself in a situation in which you are taking a huge load of classes and are struggling to get all the assignments done, then either drop one class or consider ways to make some sacrifices. For a semester in my sophomore year, I was enrolled in three high-intensity production classes. I had to make a tough decision. I stuck with the course load, but spent less time on one of the classes and retained my focus on the other two.

Being the way I am, I was obsessed with my GPA. I was always determined to attain a high GPA. This semester taught me that grades weren't everything. I was in college to learn, not accumulate points like air miles. I ended up surviving the term.

The Upside of Most College Professors

Many teachers, particularly at large universities, are adjunct faculty. This means they are not full-time. In some instances, they may even have a job outside of teaching. I have found that adjunct professors can be valuable connections to the work world. One teacher that I was very close to in college offered me an internship at his business. I learned a lot more from the internship than I did in the classroom.

I have found that most adjunct faculty members were more laid back and easy going than many full-time professors. Being an Aspie, I work a lot better with teachers who are more casual and even-tempered. I lack the talent of reading the subtleties of personalities. Some of the tenured professors I had in college were intense and uncompromising. As a result, I struggled in their classes. For an Aspie, a person who behaved in a fierce manner never made sense to me. In those classes, I just completed the assignments to get by.

When I transferred to my four-year school, I discovered that graduate students often taught freshman-level courses. This was a bit of shock for me; I was under the assumption that college teachers were older. However, I felt more relaxed around graduate students than full-time professors. I think part of this was because of the age difference. My basic German teacher was only a few years older than me. I felt like she was an older sister that I never had. This sort of connection helped ease my anxiety in her class. I did not feel the barrier with her that I did with other tenured professors. Like adjunct faculty members, graduate students are good people to keep in contact with. They could become a friend or even require your assistance for a project that pays.

I learned in college that the old phrase, "Those who can't do, teach," is not a fair statement. Some of my professors left their jobs in television or animation because they wanted to become teachers. These individuals have a passion for what they do.

Some teachers I had did not require a textbook for the class. This depended on the type of class it was, of course. For instance, my studio classes rarely required a textbook, whereas liberal arts courses did. Production-oriented classes were the most fun for me. Rather than forcing the class into memorization of principles, they gave us opportunities for hands-on learning.

One of the best courses I ever took in college was 3D modeling. When the professor assigned a book, it was only used as a reference in case the students wanted to create a tornado or blow up a house (virtually, of course). This professor would be on my list of my five most inspiring college teachers. This professor became a real mentor and a friend for my final two years at the community college.

During your school experience, you will probably find at least one individual who will impact you in a positive way. I have been fortunate to meet so many of them over the years. I hope you do as well.

The Downside of Some College Professors

I included the word "some" in the above title because poor teachers are fewer than the good. Nevertheless, it is worth discussing some of the unpleasant personalities and traits you might encounter. Some teachers have what I deem as an elitist, or exhibiting a my-way-or-the-highway attitude. This is not necessarily a bad thing, but it can get nasty if you do not abide by their rules. Being an Aspie, this was usually not a problem for me. However, I had one teacher I did not get along with. In one instance during a night class, I forgot to turn off my cell phone. It suddenly rang when he was talking. He looked right at me and shouted, "Will you please turn that thing off?!"

I flipped open the phone and closed it, completely disregarding who had called. I admit that it was a bad mistake on my part to forget to silence the ringer, but I did not like how the teacher handled the situation. He singled me out in front of the entire class. I felt small and on edge for the rest of that course.

Other professors you might encounter can be closed-minded or prejudiced against people, specifically individuals with disabilities. This never became an issue for me. I did have a few teachers who were very sarcastic. While sarcasm can be used for humor, it is often condescending. Being a person with Asperger's, it is difficult for me to identify sarcasm. I can more or less tell if someone is joking by his inflection. The same professor who singled me out used a lot of sarcasm in his lectures. One time, he poked fun at me at the start of a class session.

"Look here, there's Jeff Kraus, sitting in the exact same spot as he has for the entire semester," he exclaimed. "Are you going to sit anywhere else other than the left seat in the front row?"

I did not know how to react. I was mortified. The class chuckled. I ended up just shrugging the whole thing off. Looking back now, I can identify that he was just joking around. At the time though, I did not know that he was being sarcastic.

College professors are usually not bullies; they do not have the time or interest to make your life miserable. It is a guarantee that you will find unlikable people in your life. Some may just happen to be teachers.

Another professor I had did not teach his classes. Instead, he gave out tutorial packets for us to figure out. He always seemed irritated when a student asked him a question. He often told the class to refer to the packet for the answer. The problem was that the packets did not usually answer our questions. I always held the notion that when a student is confused, the teacher is there to help. For some reason, this professor did not see it that way. Faculty members have different teaching styles. You need to know what works best for you.

The unfortunate thing about unlikable college teachers, particularly ones in your major, is that you are stuck with them. I have found several ways to deal with these kinds of professors. First, before you enroll in a course, I recommend visiting ratemyprofessor.com. On that site, you can search a teacher's name and check out their rating as well as any available comments. However, you need to take the comments on this site with a grain of salt. Former students can easily sign up for the site and write nasty, untrue things about a cool teacher. If you mostly find negative reviews, though, it is fair to conclude he is not the best.

A second option is to approach the teacher and express your concerns. A simple conversation might help resolve any animosity or problems. You might be surprised to find that he will work with you or it could backfire. You won't know until you try. Do not meet with the teacher at the start of class; wait until class dismisses. Never become violent or mouth back—those are the worst things you can do.

If talking with the teacher does not work out, see if other professors teach the same course. Classes are frequently broken up into sections taught by different faculty members. This will give you an opportunity to take the class from a different teacher. In my college experience, I was able to avoid difficult professors using this technique. However, this meant taking the class at a different time than I had hoped. You will quickly learn which teachers fit your learning style and which ones do not. Reporting the professor to the school dean is another option (but I would only do this as a last resort).

Note to Parents: Dealing with Teachers

My mother only came in once to talk with a teacher. This was when I had been facing a rough patch in one of my core classes. I had trouble expressing my worries with the professor. While college teachers have no problems meeting with parents, they prefer to talk with their students directly. Most professors view their undergraduates as mature adults who can handle their own issues. Their attitude is different than what you will find from high school teachers.

If things go sour with a teacher, like when your autism-related child reports abuse or bullying, this is when you should intervene. Talk with your AS child about how the teacher has mistreated him and choose the next course of action. However, I advise against confronting the teacher. It will only antagonize him and it will not reflect well on your child's stay at the college. Instead, I suggest going to the school dean to report the professor's unbecoming behavior. Worst-case scenario, your child can withdraw from the college and enroll in another one (again, I advise this as a last resort).

Attending a parent-teacher meeting or an open house is a good way to connect with your AS child's professors. At these events, you can see and learn what type of individuals they are. Every spring semester at the university I attended, the head of the school department held such events. Participating in these events proved a positive and enlightening experience for me. I got a chance to bond and learn about my teachers outside of the school setting. Such events can be fun for your AS child. Knowing teachers as people and feeling comfortable around them can make a big difference for your child.

Chapter 7

College Study Tips & the Classroom Environment

I always viewed studying as an objective; it was something I had to complete. With my Asperger's, paying attention to detail while reading or listening was never a problem. However, all the details and data the professors went over proved a challenge for me. I had to decide what was important to study and what was not. This proved especially problematic in the classroom where teachers lectured non-stop for one to three hours. I often did not have a clue what to write down. This is probably a problem shared by all students. However, I have found ways to deal with this frustration.

In-Class Note-Taking

I quickly learned that writing down every single word the teacher said was not feasible. I always wrote shorthand, in phrases and simple words to trigger my memory. Many of my professors regurgitated what was covered in the assigned readings. In fact, one of my history professors did this. Rarely did I take any notes in her class, since everything she said was in the book.

A laptop does help you to quickly type notes. You can catch more details and facts that teachers will cover in their lectures. What has helped me the most, though, was knowing how the professor taught her class. The college instructors I had mostly used three teaching methods: PowerPoint, overhead projectors, and straight lecture. If your teacher presents with PowerPoint, ask if you can get a copy of the file. I had many professors use the college website to post course documents, notes, grades, and even exams. One of my teachers encouraged his class to use our laptops to follow along with the PowerPoints.

Taking notes, even if it is a topic already covered in previous readings and assignments, is not a bad idea. I have found that doing this has helped me understand the material. How you take notes and what you write down are up to you. What you need to focus on is different for each class. For example, in history courses, the focus will be on people, terminology, and dates. In a social science course like economics, the elements of importance are principles, terminology, and concepts. You adapt your note-taking strategies to the material at hand.

An alternative method would be to record the teacher's lecture. This works on two conditions. First, you must have the teacher's approval. Second, this might be an accommodation provided for you through disability services. During my freshman year, I tried this technique. At first, playing the teacher's words back helped me catch details I had missed. However, listening to the entire lecture more than once was an inefficient use of time. I found very few things that I missed in my notes, so I discontinued this practice.

You will discover quickly what the teacher tests on or finds important on your first test. Thus, you can tailor your note-taking to that teacher's class. You want to consider using the services of a student note-taker if you feel like you are struggling. While I used a student's notes in my freshman year, I also took my own notes. The note-taker's notes were an extra reference for me in case I missed something.

If your teacher talks fast or skims over topics too quickly, ask him to slow down or repeat what he has said. Some professors may prefer to answer questions at the end of the lecture. If this is the case, hold your thoughts until the Q&A or mark down on a sheet of paper what questions you may have, and ask them when the teacher is ready.

Never be afraid to ask what will be on the midterms and finals. Several teachers I had in college reviewed the material prior to the exam. This proved ample coverage for me to formulate a study guide. One professor I had actually put the test on an overhead projector, giving us a chance to be perfectly ready. No one ever failed his classes.

If you get a professor as swell as this, then you are in luck beyond measure. Make it a habit of always asking your teachers for this kind of information. You may be surprised what they will provide.

Study Tips: Reading Assignments

During my high school years, teachers required the class to read one thick textbook over the entire school year. In college, professors assigned one or more books for the class to read within a 10- to 15-week semester. My average reading for each college class per week was between 20 to 50 pages. As a full-time student, this added up to 80 or more pages a week.

I quickly learned to never read the material once or wait until the night before the exam. If I waited until the last day to study, the information left my brain just as quickly as it entered. One of my college professors highlighted an important point during one of his lectures: "One of my former students told me that he worked best under pressure." He then went on to say, "Really, this is a way of saying 'I am lazy and ready to fail.'"

A more efficient study habit I have found was spreading the assigned readings over the course of the week. Like with in-class note-taking, focus on terminology, people's names, principles/concepts, dates, and other noteworthy material. This is when the highlighter comes in handy. When you find information that seems important or relevant to a test question, highlight it. Now, it might be tempting to highlight every single word in your book. I did this in my first semester in college. It made studying impossible. Instead, focus on text that is important to the subject matter. For example, if you need to read about the American Revolution, pay attention to the facts, terminology, and dates.

Another thing to consider while reading a college textbook is watching for chapter subheadings. Most of the time, books are organized like this (including the one you are reading right now). You may find one or two of the following things helpful. Keep a note card with you and write down the chapter subheadings. This can be an effective method for remembering your assigned readings. I would not recommend writing a ton of notes on the card. Copying what you read in a book is a waste of time. That's why you should highlight the text instead. In essence, the textbook becomes your study guide.

The other thing you can do is turn chapter headings into questions. For example, if your economics textbook has a section heading called "Supply and Demand," write under the subheading, "What is Supply and Demand?" Then, highlight the answers to that question in the paragraphs that follow. I used this technique through most of my college experience. I found it very helpful to my study habits.

If studying is a hefty challenge for you, I encourage you to find either a tutor or check out the college study center. During my first term in college, I found a department that was dedicated to helping students improve their study skills. I met with a lady there who showed me some of the tips I have mentioned in this book.

The community college I attended had a math department dedicated to assisting students with algebra, geometry, calculus, and special topics in mathematics. The department I found myself visiting the most was the English division. Starting out as a freshman, I never felt entirely comfortable with my writing. Setting up appointments in advance, I met with one of the tutors. They covered various issues, such as proper MLA formatting, footnotes, structure, and grammar. You will be writing many papers in college. It does not matter if you're a journalism major or a fine arts major; writing is an essential skill in higher education.

Many past teachers have told me that the amount of time you study alone does not dictate your grade. This was a hard concept for my Aspie mind to fathom. I always had equated the amount of hours I studied to my success. This proved false when I studied for five hours on a quiz that I earned a D- for. The concept that studying smart is better than studying hard rings true. Use your highlighter, catch the important facts, and understand the whole picture. You don't need to know every single word in your textbook to do well on your tests.

As a person with Asperger's, highlighting and writing inside textbooks were new experiences for me. During high school, the textbooks were provided for me by the school, while I had to get my own in college. As a result, these books were mine. I could do whatever I wanted with the book, including writing down notes or underlining important information.

Taking breaks, even short ones, during extended study sessions has allowed my mind to process the newly acquired information. If I studied non-stop, my mind encountered data overload. In turn, I could not remember the material. Spreading my study time throughout the week also helped me avoid this mental overload.

I recommend limiting yourself to no more than three hours of studying a day. If you are enrolled in four classes, allow yourself 45 minutes of study time for each class every day, include weekends, if necessary. This time management technique works incredibly well if you have to register for a foreign language course. Learning a new language is another feat itself. Practicing and memorizing words every day instills the repetition you need to master a new language.

Quizzes and Exams: Being Smart

I took my first quiz in my second week of college and earned a 60 percent. Fortunately, the class dropped the lowest quiz score, but I had used up my one lifeline. Surprisingly, this ended up being the lowest score I earned for the class. You may find yourself in a scenario where you do poorly on quizzes, especially the first couple.

Being an Aspie, I found failure unacceptable. However, I learned how to prepare for future quizzes after failing my first one. For one, it showed me what types of questions I would be asked on other tests like multiple choice, short answer, or true and false types. From this, I learned how questions would be worded or phrased on future tests. Teachers are often repetitive in their testing methods. Some professors prefer multiple-choice questions, while others favor blue books and essays. Finally, a failed quiz demonstrated how hard the rest of them could be, whether I needed to study more or not.

As highlighted in the previous section, teachers love to focus their test questions on word definitions and principles. Keep an eye out for bolded or italicized terminology in your textbooks.

I will point out that open-note tests can actually be more difficult than closed-note test. This may sound preposterous. If you're allowed to use your notes or better yet your book, what could go wrong? In the public speaking course I took, all the tests were open book. The professor gave us a whole class period to finish the test. His exams were the hardest I ever encountered. No one ever aced his exams. Studying the material but also knowing how he drafted his test questions helped me significantly. By the end of the term, I set a new high grade standard in his class.

Students may think that since notes or books are allowed on some tests, there is no need to study. In turn, they find themselves spending a lot of time flipping through their books to locate the answer to each question instead of actually knowing any information from studying. In my opinion, this is why closed-note tests are much easier. As a person with Asperger's, I knew I had to study. The challenge in college was knowing what to study. This did not lessen my anxiety with the transition from high school to college.

If you have a teacher who gives open-note or open-book tests, make a point to study as if it were closed note. Gather your notes and formulate cheat sheet for the terms or principles you have trouble understanding. When I took Micro Economics 101, the professor permitted the class to use a two-sided 3 x 5 note card. I crammed in all the graphs and principles I could in that small piece of paper for the exams. Keep your notes only as a reference. Do not rely on them to pass the test.

Do not try to remember every detail of your assigned readings. This is not feasible. It is better to have a general overview of each chapter. Again, keep an eye out for important words, phrases, or principles. You won't remember everything, and there is no shame in not achieving this kind of goal.

If you don't know an answer to a question, skip it and move on. Go through the whole test, answering the questions you know and then track back to the ones you are uncertain about. For a long time, my Asperger's mind forced me to answer test questions in the order they were presented. I always felt that everything had to be completed in a specific order or method. This is not true for tests. I could answer question number 15 first if I really wanted to.

When I scour through a test, I generally mark a period or a star against a question I am confused on. I answer these questions last. This method has saved me a lot of time. I did not feel pressured by the clock if I answered questions 5 to 20 but not 1 to 4. There is nothing wrong with acting on a gut instinct either, especially if you don't know the answer to a question. Apply logic and think about how answer A makes much more sense than answer B.

Never be afraid to raise your hand if you take your test in the class. While your professor cannot give you the answer, she can certainly clarify what the question asks. When I took my yearlong sequence of foreign language, I quickly found myself disadvantaged by taking the tests at disability services. I had no one to help me on questions that confused me. Because of that, I did poorly on the first two tests.

Before the third exam, I approached my teacher and asked her if I could take the next test in class. She told me it would not be a problem. If I needed extra time, I could finish it up in the department office under her supervision. When I received my third exam, I smiled upon seeing my greatly improved grade. I have found that many teachers will work with their students.

The final and most important study tip I can offer you is to get enough sleep. I knew too many former classmates who functioned on only 3 to 4 hours of sleep per night. I have no idea how they achieved this. I assume they relied on a lot of caffeine. Don't go through college this way. In the long haul, it will backfire.

If you choose to use a tape recorder during class lectures, I recommend playing it as you go to sleep. I don't know the science behind this, but when you hear the teacher's voice while you sleep, the subconscious part of your mind is still awake. Ideally, this may help you retain more information.

Quizzes and Exams: The Three Formats to Look out For

Tests and exams are just like the others you have taken in junior high and high school. They mainly consist of true/false, multiple choice, and essay questions. I will examine the main testing formats that colleges use for students as well as provide a break down on how you can prepare yourself for them.

True/False and Multiple-Choice Tests

For the record, I completely loathe true/false questions. It grinds my gears when a professor throws in an element that is true, but then continues the question with a part that feels iffy or possibly false. More likely than not, you have encountered a true/false question like this. When answering these types of questions, the statement must be entirely true. There is no middle ground. If you don't know the answer, that's when going with your gut comes into play. Answering a true/false question means you have a 50/50 chance of getting it right.

For multiple-choice questions, if you don't know the answer to the question, the odds of getting it right are reduced. Some people say that if you don't know, pick either letter B or C, because choice letters A and D are rarely the answer on multiple-choice tests. However, one of my college professors debunked this myth. He gave our class a test with only multiple-choice questions. Looking at the first question, I saw that the answer was letter A. Moving to the next one the answer was also A. The same rang true for the next three questions. When I had finished the test, every single answer was the first letter choice. In a nutshell, the exam was an easy A. So, no, do not put down B or C if you don't know the answer. Go with what you feel is the right answer.

Essay Exams

Essays will most likely show up at some point during your college experience. As an Aspie student, these were the easiest tests for me to take in college. Unlike true/false or multiple-choice questions, essays do not require pure memorization or regurgitation of course readings and material. They gave me a chance to express the answer in my own words.

Though most of your teachers will want you to write out your answers on the test, some may request an item called the "Blue Book," an item I referenced a few sections back. This is a small pamphlet full of lined paper, designed for students to write extended essays. Blue Books reflect a kind of old-school approach, yet they may pop up every now and then. Do not be surprised if your professor requires one.

When I enrolled in a yearlong sequence of American history, my professor told the class to buy several books for our exams. She did not believe in multiple-choice or true/false questions. Our essays could be as long as we wanted. However, our answers were to be long, yet clear and explanatory to the topic. We also needed to use sources for our answers. Fortunately, she gave the essays out in advance for us to study.

I may not be a typical Aspie, but I have several intense interests that border on obsession. One of them happened to be American history. If you're really focused on a particular subject, you could enroll in courses that relate to that interest. As a result, you could find yourself doing exceedingly well in such classes. In this class, I wrote answers that were several pages long for the essays. I ended up doing well on all of this teacher's exams.

Online Tests vs. Paper

Many colleges have really transitioned to the use of the Internet for just about everything: class enrollment, degree audits, scholarship submissions, course schedules, and even tests. For every course I took in college, I either had to submit a paper online or complete an Internet-based exam.

I have found that online tests are a bit different and somewhat beneficial in comparison to pencil-and-paper exams. You can take them at your leisure and in a suitable environment, outside the classroom. You can even glance at your notes or class book. After all, the teacher won't be supervising you during an online test.

There are a few caveats, though. One relates to the power of your Internet connection. If you lose it, then you can be logged out of the school site, which means you will be unable to finish the test. This happened to me once during my freshman year. I sent an email to the professor describing the situation, and he was able to reset the test so I could take it again. This is an easy solution to this kind of problem.

The other thing you will frequently encounter with online tests is that they are usually timed. Being an Aspie, this was a bit stressful for me. My extended testing time was also applied to Internet-based tests. These quizzes run on a clock. In my opinion, there is something not right about seeing a countdown while I'm taking test. It's like watching a ticking time bomb. It took me practice to ignore this distraction. Rather than constantly checking and concerning myself over how much time I had left, I set a post-it note over the clock. Then I kept my focus on answering the questions. Have your notes and book on standby if that makes you feel better and more confident.

Like pencil-and-paper tests, online exams require you to finish them in one setting. For a 20-minute quiz, that's not a big deal.

However, for an exam with 50 or more questions, that can be somewhat of challenge. I had one teacher who gave three online exams for the course of the term. These tests covered anywhere from 6-10 chapters. Her exams were usually over 100 questions. On average, counting bathroom breaks, it took me three hours to complete these tests. The desire to glance at my book constantly drove me nuts during each exam.

I hope you won't have to endure such a test, they are brutal. If you do run into them, be ready for a long haul. As the teacher told her class on day one, "If you have not read the book, you will have when you finish my exams."

Class Presentations

Public speaking is a skill that colleges encourage and instill in their students. I have not met a professor who did not assign a class presentation. Standing before a group of people can be a nerve-racking experience. For a long time, I loathed speaking in front of others. I remember intentionally missing class presentation day in high school because of my fear of standing in front of others. My face grew hot. Sweat ran down my back. And my mind would take an escape route to la-la land.

Enrolling in an effective public speaking course during my sophomore year of college freed me from this anxiety. Like it or not, talking in front of others is mandatory, especially in the work world. No person can live as a clam or remain isolated from others. Being able to communicate with people is critical. If you are required to enroll in a public speaking course, I have some beginner's advice that can hopefully get you on your way.

The old trick of staring at the back of the classroom does not work. As my effective public speaking teacher once said, "Speakers need to keep constant eye contact with their subjects to build a level of intimacy and interest."

For a person with Asperger's, making eye contact is like telling a bird (other than a penguin) to swim. It is hard, if not downright impossible. To this day, I have trouble looking into people's eyes. I find eye contact discomforting and frankly an unnecessary way to communicate with others. However, there is a trick I use to at least give the impression that I am making eye contact with people.

When I talk to most individuals, I look at a particular part of their face. I often find myself looking at moles, lips, cheeks, and noses. While this method may not seem practical or even correct by most, it was how I started. Looking at someone's face shows that you are not rude or overly shy. This takes lots of practice. It all started when I tried this with friends and family.

After practicing this method with people I was comfortable around, I then applied it to everyone else. Try it first with a close family member, and then broaden this technique to other people. Bit by bit, you can use this technique on other individuals. As an Aspie, I only make eye contact with people I know well or with someone who is important, like an employer or a professor. During long conversations, though, I still find myself drifting back to the mouth or nose, or sometimes away from the person.

When talking to a group of people, make sure to look from one face to another. Do not stare at one person. If you do that, you might creep that guy (or girl) out. Glancing at everyone's faces shows your general interest in the group.

While using notes in an oral presentation, do not carry large sheets of paper and read from them. PowerPoint and note cards are better ways to go. With note cards, only write down simple ideas to prompt your memory on the topic. This means you need to practice what you want to say. Either present it at home in front of a mirror or use a camera to record your performance. Using the latter option gives you a chance to point out your mistakes and make efforts to improve upon them. Practice your presentation at least five times a day. Anything less than that and you will start forgetting things.

The best way to approach a presentation is to view the task as though you are an actor on a stage. You are in front of an audience with which you share something important. Instead of reciting Shakespeare, you are delivering information. Make the performance your own. Use your note cards and PowerPoint as props instead of crutches. They are tools, not your lifelines.

Remember, students are not there to gawk or make fun of you. They are too busy studying for their classes to engage in such childish antics. Besides, the other students in class are going to be right where you're standing very soon.

Classrooms

The image of a traditional high school room, filled with 20 individualized desks and a whiteboard, does not always reflect the college experience. During my first term, I had two classes in an auditorium, another one in a pavilion, and the last one in a computer lab. The classes varied in size, structure, and location, which made transitioning incredibly hard for me. I found scouting the locations of all my classes in advance to be very helpful. Doing this became sort of an adventure, particularly when I transferred to a large university. Enrolled in fourteen credit hours, I had to walk to several different buildings on campus. For my first class, the quickest on-foot route averaged 12 minutes. My on-campus journeys were like traveling through a small city within an urban setting. Being an Aspie, I methodically explored different routes, determining which one would get me to my classes the fastest.

Time is very important to me. I nearly drove my parents insane when I timed short trips around our community. I would then compare trips one day to the next, informing them which route was quicker. In college, this obsession continued. I had to get to my classes on time. Once I had found the quickest route, it became part of my routine to class. Breaks between classes were essential for me. They gave me time to get to class. Once I arrived, I had a chance to transition my mind to the material of the next course.

During one semester, I made the mistake of scheduling only a ten-minute window between two classes. Jogging across campus became the norm. It was a stressful experience. Make sure to plan a schedule that works for you.

As for the classrooms themselves, make sure you locate a seat that gives you a good view of the teacher. If you have a class in a large auditorium, this can be tricky. Assigned seating does not exist in college. Early arrivals get the best spots. I always tried to reach my classes 10 minutes early to get the premium seat locations. You will find in college that most students do not pick the front row seats. In just about every class I enrolled in, students usually sat in the back or middle sections. Rarely did they take the front row. I have no idea why this was the case. I can only gather that most students did not want to be in the teacher's line of sight.

With Asperger's, I found that the front row seats were ideal for me. I grew up sitting at the end of the front row throughout school. Up front, I could hear and see the teacher clearly. I don't like distractions, which tend to be more prominent the further back you sit in the classroom. Sitting in the front row was a familiar part of my old routine, and it eliminated a transition obstacle for me. My attention was on the teacher, and I usually did not pick up on the distractions behind me.

As a quick note about auditoriums, not all of them are designed to carry perfect acoustics. Picking out a professor's voice in a large room may prove very challenging, especially if hearing is not your strongest sense. Unlike high school, modifications cannot be made in the classroom. You are stuck with the room that the class is assigned to. If there is a fan or a heater that keeps rattling, there is nothing you can do about it.

With my Asperger's, I pick up on sounds that most people do not notice. I sat in one classroom where the fluorescent lights kept buzzing. Such noises are distracting and frankly annoy the heck out of me. Only after time have I been able to blot out these sounds by forcing my attention to another detail in the room like a whiteboard or a window. Sitting up front and focusing on the teacher does help me to block out such noises.

If soft, environmental sounds are a problem for you, I recommend wearing earphones. Before the beginning of each class, I entered the room with my iPod and listened to music. When class began, I removed the headphones. The purpose of this exercise was to calm my mind. Hearing repetitive melodies and sounds helps tame my sensitive senses. To this day, I listen to music before going to bed. It resets my brain to sleep mode, as it did for study time.

When I got older, another technique that worked for me was intentionally taking note of the background noises. When listening to a repetitive sound, my mind became accustomed to its rhythm, like a fan running or a car engine roaring. White noises like these can be annoying on a first encounter. However, when you allow yourself some time to listen to them, they can transition seamlessly from a distraction to a background sound.

This is a weird phenomenon I can't really explain. Listening to the same sound repeatedly tricks the mind. The brain no longer views the sound as important, thus registering it out completely. I am sure there are psychological or maybe even scientific studies on this topic. However, I'm not going to delve into them here, since that is not the purpose of this book.

One more note, if you arrive to your class early, consider sitting in different areas of the room. Doing this gives you a chance to find the locations of any distracting sounds. If need be, you can adjust to a different area where the sounds are less troublesome.

Notes to Parents: Helping Your Child Adjust

The transition into higher education is a HUGE task. Your AS child may encounter some stressful moments or even face complete meltdowns. When one of my college professors assigned a hundred pages worth of reading for the first week of class, I flipped out. I found myself in my parents' family room, ranting on how demanding and unrealistic the teacher was for handing out such a ludicrous amount of homework.

"Why would he do this to us?" I shouted. "Does he want us to fail?"

"Probably not," my father said matter-of-factly. "Teachers do this on purpose to weed out the slackers from the dedicated students. You will be fine. You are a good student."

His words rang true. By the third week of the term, half the class had dropped the course. This is common, especially among undecided majors and freshmen who are getting a feel for which program is the right fit for them. A little encouragement goes a long way. If your AS child needs help, be proactive, but not a helicopter parent.

Remember, college is all about your child's growth in education and his extension into the real world.

Early on in my freshman year, I asked my father to join me on some of my class projects. He obliged and helped me immensely on one of my photography courses. On weekends, he became my subject as I snapped away photos both within the school studio and at outdoor locations. In a way, this brought us a bit closer. Being the photographer nut that he is, I ended up enlightening him on the terms and principles he had learned long ago.

I am not saying you have to get this involved in your AS child's college projects. Simply being present can be a real blessing for your child. My mother never listened in on the college essays I had written, but her objective perspective on topics enhanced my writing capabilities. I thank her for her huge contributions to the many successes in my life.

Aside from potentially being a stand-in for projects and serving as an editor, you may also want to consider asking your child if he needs a quiz giver. On multiple occasions, my dad would go through my photography textbook and ask me questions like "what is the rule-of-thirds principle?" I would give him an answer, and he would tell me if I was right or wrong. Setting a little time aside like this can be beneficial for your AS child.

Chapter 8

Commuting &
On-Campus Life

Where you live and how you travel to class are very important factors when transitioning to college. Will you be living in a dorm or off-campus in an apartment? Will you be commuting to school every day? Though only you can decide which domicile would work best to your advantage, I have outlined some benefits and caveats of each approach.

Living On-Campus: The Advantages

There are some universities who require students to live on campus. Such a prerequisite may make this decision easier if moving to a dorm seems reasonable to your personal preference. Living on campus provides many advantages. An on-campus experience offers a communal environment in which you are surrounded by people your age, specifically individuals who share your interests, and this makes friendship building very easy. Living on campus gives you the flexibility to hang out with people and not face the frustration of getting stuck in traffic on your way to school.

There is also the matter of convenience. On-campus living means you are always walking distance to class and school events. This works particularly well for those dreadful 8:00 AM courses. You don't have to wake up early to commute or pay for parking.

Living on campus can offer more individuality and self-reliance versus living at home with your family. You get to do your own laundry, buy your own food, and handle your own expenses. In a way, living in a dorm can be viewed as a huge step into adulthood.

Living On-Campus: The Disadvantages

College costs can nearly double when you add on-campus housing and living expenses. Out-of-state tuition for state universities is even more expensive. If you are relying on student loans, the money you receive can be diverted from tuition to housing costs. This means you may end up with more student debt.

Another feature worth mentioning is the potentially non-study-friendly atmosphere you could potentially find in a college dorm. You could have loud and obnoxious neighbors. The stereotype of the unreliable, buffoonish roommate in so many comedic movies could become your reality. I am not implying that this will happen during your on-campus experience. However, it very well can. You do not get to choose your roommate. You are stuck with whomever you get, and you and your roommate may not be compatible.

Privacy is almost non-existent in dorms. As a general rule for most colleges, two to four students are required to share a room. You can request to have a room for yourself, but that is unlikely to be granted. Being diagnosed with Asperger's, I prefer to wind down after a full day in a controlled, quiet environment. Living with someone you do not know can be an unsettling experience. You may find yourself living in libraries a lot more than in your dorm.

Now, I am not trying to deter you from choosing to live on campus. It will be another transition that you will undertake. I chose to stay at home and commute. I grew up in a very quiet and stable household, and I felt that moving to a new environment would have compounded the anxieties of studying at a large university.

Living on Your Own: The Good and the Bad

There are many benefits to this housing option. For one, you could have a place near campus to live, which makes traveling to class much more convenient. You can obtain some independence. But this comes with huge responsibilities. You have to balance a budget. Food, rent, electricity, and other utilities add up to hundreds, if not over a thousand dollars per month.

You may need one or more roommates to share the costs.

You might need to get a job in order to keep the apartment afloat. Laundry, vacuuming, cleaning, and handling bills can add more hours to your life than you may have available, especially if you are enrolled in a demanding college program. As an Aspie college student, all the complexities of finding an apartment and sharing the bills were too much for me. It is hard enough to become accustomed to a new school environment without adding the stress of renting a home.

Living at Home: The Advantages

Living at home was the best option for me. Being an Aspie, I have difficulty with transitioning. Going to the community college brought me the shock factor. Upon my arrival at the university, I almost went into a sensory overload. It took time for me to adjust to these new environments. Large college campuses are a new world in and of themselves.

Commuting to college from home eased my mind. Knowing that I could sleep in my own childhood bed was a real comfort. Staying with my parents also helped settle my anxious mind throughout college. They provided me a support system that I don't think I could have found if I lived in a dorm or on my own. I was fortunate to stay at home, yet I had my own personal space. This arrangement only works if you live within driving distance from your college.

Living at Home: The Disadvantages

When I enrolled for my undergraduate degree, the university was 25 miles away. Every day, five days a week, I drove an average of 50 miles. I put over 1,000 miles on my truck each month. I spent more time than usual at gas pumps and auto maintenance shops.

In addition, the university charged commuter students parking fees. The cost of a parking pass was anywhere from $200 to $500 a semester. I opted for the cheapest garage, which was always the furthest from my classes. I picked up a lot of extra walking time. As a result, I went through running shoes very quickly. This was yet another expense I had to consider when commuting to a university.

Another limitation that comes from driving to school is time. A long drive can get in the way of attending school activities. To participant in my college's activities, I had to make extra trips. Living at home also became an obstacle to building friendships. The university I attended had a community-based environment. This made it convenient for on-campus students to meet up with friends on short notice.

In my situation, I had to plan social gatherings in advance because of the distance I had to travel. I learned that, within the university lifestyle, hardly anything is ever really thought out or planned. Friendships and meetings just happen. You never know who you will meet or when you will see a friend again, unless you share a class with that individual. I met some very good friends over the years from just being in class with them. When the semester ended, it was difficult for me to keep in touch with old pals. As an Aspie, this frustrated me to no end. It was nearly impossible for me to adapt to the unstructured, carefree social environment of the university. A college friend finally told me, "Don't fret about things. Just go with the flow."

The Final Decision ...

The decision is yours to make regarding where you will live. You have to do what is best for you. If the school you are enrolled in is hundreds of miles away from your parents' home, you will need to live on campus or in a nearby apartment. If the school is within driving range, I encourage you to stay at home. Keep your options open. A convenient location should not be the reason you enroll in a specific college.

Your decision does not have to be final. You may want to consider living at home for a while and then move on campus for the remainder of your schooling. During this time, you will discover your preferred lifestyle, like whether you enjoy living with people or alone. While I would not say this is common, it is an option.

College Parking

Parking can be an unwieldy experience. When I first got my parking pass at the university, I began to wonder how I could turn it in once the semester had finished. The lady at the parking services' desk told me to drop it off in the office. This brought up a new question. If I had to turn my pass into the parking services office, where would I park when I had to turn the pass in? Does that mean I had to pay to park for that one extra day after spending $200 to $300 a semester for parking?

At the university I attended, a person could enter a garage without a pass but had to pay a fee when he left. There was no fee if a person stayed for less than 15 minutes. If an individual stayed on campus for over three hours, the cost hit the maximum of ten dollars. On the final day of every semester, I used my pass for my last long visit, and then I would exit the garage.

I drove around the block and re-entered the garage. At the kiosk, I clicked the "I have no pass" option. The machine spat out a little piece of paper, which I kept on my dashboard. I parked my vehicle and ran to parking services to return my pass. Then I ran back to my vehicle in order to exit the garage within 15 minutes, for free. My quickest time to achieve this ridiculous activity was under five minutes. It wasn't until later that I found a drop off box for returning passes. This container was right at the garage exit. It turns out I had done all this hard work for nothing.

As an Aspie, I followed the parking employees' instructions literally and didn't look for other options. During all the times I entered and left the garage, I did not even notice the drop-off box. This is why you need to do your research on your school's parking garages to see if there are drop-off points for parking passes. The other thing you must watch out for are the dates when the passes become available. Obtaining your parking pass as early as possible is essential. There are a limited number of parking passes, and they are quickly sold.

Parking is not always a hassle. The same time I received my university student ID at the community college, I picked up a pass at no charge. All I had to do was set the pass under my visor to identify my truck as a student vehicle. Students were designated to park in the white-lined spots. The yellow parking lines were for faculty. In this way, college parking can be a bit rigid.

I remember pulling into the community college's parking lot on the first day of school. It was 8:45 AM, and every single spot in the front lot was full. Being an Aspie who is obsessed with being on time, I looked for the nearest spot. The closest one I found was handicapped parking. Only thinking about getting to class on time, I pulled into the handicapped spot. At ten o'clock that night, I walked to my truck and found a note under my windshield. It was a warning from school security. Though I did not receive a ticket, I learned my lesson.

There was nothing I could do when the parking lots filled up. I solved this problem by arriving to class a half hour earlier than usual. This allowed me to find a decent parking place. Also, it gave me some extra time to prepare for class and relax my mind.

Alternative Transportation

Since I attended a large university, the school offered bus transportation for students. If I attended one campus and needed to reach another campus, I could get a free ride to that building. You may want to look into this option if driving is not your forte. This only works on one condition: the bus schedule must coincide with your class times. You are often at the mercy of the bus drivers. Even though buses are required to arrive and depart on time, they rarely do. The hours are not very flexible, either.

As an Aspie, it irks me that buses don't stick to their schedules. At the school I attended, the bus schedule started as late as 9:00 AM and ran only until 8:00 PM. This put students with early-morning and evening classes at a huge disadvantage. Check your school bus schedules before considering this option.

The other thing you can look into is catching a ride from a close friend or a family member. On a couple of occasions, I asked my dad to drive me to class and back. These instances worked out better at the community college, since its location was less than a mile from my father's office. During my final year there, I ended up giving a friend of mine lifts from his house and back for a semester. This option can work, but again, it only really works out when the campus is in close proximity to your home.

Note to Parents: Driving and Other Means of Schooling

Adjusting to a new school is a challenge, especially when commuting. Driving is a huge responsibility. Living in a dorm or on your own poses even bigger challenges. Lay out all the plans and review the options available and guide your AS child through this maze. It is possible that she is not ready for such a huge transition.

My first few weeks in college were complete train wrecks; I did not know the environment. I was also unfamiliar with morning and evening traffic jams. As an Aspie, I am not overly fond of loud horns and tight spaces, and traffic jams usually present both. I do not like being late, either. On one occasion, the interstate was at a standstill. I sat in the left lane, nervously tapping my steering wheel. I glanced over at my clock. It read 8:48 AM. Class started in twelve minutes. I had been stuck in traffic for nearly an hour. Out of the corner of my eye, I saw a metro bus flying down the outermost lane, along the divider. Thinking it was a good idea at the time, I followed the bus until half a mile from my exit.

Being Asperger's, I like to find the quickest solution. I did not realize that driving on the outermost lane was illegal action. Safety comes first. It is better to be late for class than cause an accident or get cited for a traffic violation.

Enrolling in online courses could be a good start for your AS child. In fact, many universities offer these kinds of classes. Talk this idea over with your AS child. It can very well help her transition into the college environment. She needs to know that online classes are just as demanding as those taught in the classroom.

Living on campus can be stressful and can push your AS child way out of her comfort zone. You know your AS child's needs better than anyone. Whether she should live on campus or commute to class is your call. Guide her in making a decision that you know is in her best interest.

Chapter 9

Budget
& Food

The university I graduated from has several different stadiums, libraries, cafeterias, restaurants, stores, and even a gym. I have discovered that colleges are not just institutions for education. They offer many entertainment venues as well. It is very easy to spend the extra money for food and entertainment. To save up on costs, stick to a budget. This advice applies not only to Asperger's students, but also to anyone on their own for the first time.

Budgeting Food

Early in my college career, I sat down with my father and discussed how I should handle my food expenses. We agreed on a weekly allowance of $45. I learned to work within a fixed budget, what to buy, and what not to buy. This worked well at the community college. There was a cafeteria and three restaurants near the campus. Fast food runs became the norm. Being on campus only three times a week also helped with the expenses.

During my time at the university, $45 per week proved an unrealistic budget. I was on campus five days a week for eight to ten hours each day. I solved this as a math problem.

On average daily, I could only spend nine dollars. I did not dip into my savings to make up the shortfalls. I learned not to add side dishes to meals or turn them into combos for an extra $1.99. Restaurants, particularly fast food joints, love to up-charge customers for a drink and fries. I generally had to turn those choices down to keep within my budget.

Food service choices vary from campus to campus. For the sake of your taste buds, I recommend not going to the same place twice in one week. If you are registered in a city or state college, I advise against wandering off campus for safety reasons. The neighborhood surrounding the university I attended was not the safest in the city. If you decide to explore beyond the campus grounds, make sure you go with a group of people.

For inexpensive meals, visit fast food joints. While I have no intention to promote the Whopper (even though I enjoy eating them every now and then), they fill you up fast with calories and carbohydrates. Though not the healthiest, they make you feel full. Vending machines for soda and snacks are not too terrible either. However, watch out for caffeine-loaded drinks. You can very easily suffer a "high" or where you feel pumped up with extra energy. While this may last for a time, it is followed by a "crash," which makes you feel inactive and completely lost in a haze. You do not want this to happen while you are in class.

One time, I had to stay late for a class project. In an effort to stay awake, I bought myself a cold energy drink. I downed it within minutes. I felt like I could climb Mount Everest (figuratively speaking). An hour went by, then two. I continued to feel great and overly ecstatic. By the two and a half hour mark, my body began to shift into a totally different direction. My mind slowed down. I felt so tired that I was tempted to take a nap during the teacher's lecture (thankfully I did not). The drive home was just as exhausting. Do not do this to yourself, particularly for a night class.

Visiting walk-in stores that sell snacks is not a bad move either. Just be warned that, depending on the store, the snacks could be pricey. Health food snacks are quite expensive, sometimes costing over three dollars. You may want to consider packing snacks from home. This way you can easily grab something on the go. Also consider bringing a water bottle with you to class.

Cutting Costs When Buying Food

When you order a meal, I suggest selecting water instead of a soda. Water is usually free, and it is better for your body. Avoid extra sides unless your meal comes with one. To save even more, you may want to try eating slower. As a young college graduate, this is easier said than done. I admit it, I love eating. I often eat quickly so I can move on to the next task. However, I have taught myself to eat slower.

Doing this makes your stomach fill up quickly. Thus, you do not need to eat as much. Several of my family members use this old trick on a daily basis. Practicing this method can also help you lose weight, if that is a concern of yours.

Places you want to avoid as much as possible are coffee shops. If you are a coffee lover, this will prove difficult. Big universities are full of Starbucks shops. The lines for them in the morning and late evening are long and never seem to end. There is nothing wrong with having a latte or mocha every now and then, but living off of them night and day is not wise. Coffee is expensive. If you stick to a $9 a day budget like I did, purchasing a $4 mocha latte does not leave you much money for lunch.

There are other ways to wake up besides drinking a mug of coffee. Exercise in the morning. Eat a hearty breakfast. Follow a day-to-day wake up routine. There is nothing better than a hot shower at 7:00 AM to stir your drowsy senses.

If you live on campus, you may want to look into a monthly meal plan. Big universities have restaurants open for students to walk in, swipe their pre-paid cards, and eat breakfast, lunch, and dinner. Search your college website for dining plans. It could be a cost-effective way to get food.

You can go old school and pack your own lunch. Make sure to put your lunch in an insulated container that will keep your food at a proper temperature. You may have to buy a special container to preserve your food. An easier solution would be to pack foods that do not require refrigeration.

On-Campus Parties

Finding free food at college events is easy. One of the classes I took in my junior year had a meeting every Thursday. At these get-togethers, pizza and drinks were provided for the class. During the entire semester, I had free dinner on Thursdays. This option may not be available at your school. Nonetheless, check to see if there are any organizations that provide free food to students. Such an opportunity can fill your belly.

Placing an Order with Cashiers and Servers

Speaking with others is awkward for people with Asperger's. Whenever I went out to a restaurant with my family as a child, I could never order for myself. I always told my parents ahead of time what I wanted, and they ordered for me. It was not until my teenage years that I finally had the courage to advocate for myself. Doing so took some practice. I remember developing somewhat of a stutter as I spoke up. Feeling awkward around people became the norm for some time. To this day, I still don't feel entirely comfortable around people, whether it be strangers in a crowd or family get-togethers.

When you order food, particularly at a fast food joint, you need to know what you want. Lines are very long, especially during lunchtime. Clamming up when the cashier asks, "How may I help you?" is the worst thing that can happen in a lunch queue. Customers in line can get very agitated. They want to get their food quickly. Holding up the line will make this an unpleasant experience for you, the cashier, and everyone else. If you are uncomfortable or do not know what to order, step aside.

Once you know what you want to eat, place your order with the cashier or server. Speak clearly and loudly enough so he can hear you. A crowded cafeteria can be very noisy, whereas a café might not be. It is not mandatory to look at a person when placing your order. You give your order, pay the amount, and move on. I would not order with your head to the floor though; this could make it hard for the cashier to hear you.

If the cashier or server speaks too fast, tell him to slow down. If you are perplexed over an inquiry, ask him to repeat the question. All these conversations you have with people may be tedious and diffi-cult. I felt so awkward about it that I scripted some phrases in ad-vance, including saying, "please" and "thank you."

After you place an order, the cashier will give you the total amount to pay. If you have a meal plan, which often comes with a card, give that to him so he can swipe it. Otherwise, pay in cash or a credit card. I prefer cash or debit.

The Best Time for Food

Colleges and universities are crowded places by design. They get worse when lunchtime hits. I discovered that the typical noon to 1:00 PM lunch hour does not apply to college. I found lines that ran out of a Subway restaurant at 2:00 PM. There is no particular time for lunch, since classes dismiss at a variety of times. Being an Aspie, crowded rooms, long lines, and loud noises are almost unbearable. At both colleges I attended, I learned the crowded times for the cafeteria and restaurants at lunch.

I often had my biggest meal either before 11 AM or after 2:30 PM. I generally opted for the latter because many classes I had to take ran until 9 o'clock at night. When I did this, I easily avoided the lunch-time craze. These are things that you, as a student, need to figure out. Eating a relatively good-sized meal around 3:00 PM satisfied me for the remainder of the day. I rarely ate dinner in college. Instead, I visited vending machines for a snack and then went home at night to eat.

If you have a class at 2:00 PM or another time that interferes with a manageable lunch schedule, try to squeeze in a food run. How well you handle loud noises or crowds might be different for you. If a place is too noisy or chaotic, get out of dodge. There is no point in lingering around an area that pushes you beyond your comfort zone.

Note to Parents: Starting a Food Budget

Setting your AS child on a weekly budget is a good way to introduce him to the concept of managing money. Talk this idea over with him and agree on a realistic number. Every semester, I negotiated a weekly budget with my father. Some weeks I ended up spending more than others. Your child will certainly encounter this scenario. If the initial budget amount does not seem manageable, you may have to raise it. Do not increase the budget by much, though. The purpose of this exercise is to teach your AS child the value of currency. This is an important lesson your teen needs to grasp as he moves onto life outside of school.

Don't make this another big concern for your AS child; she will have enough on her mind with college. Once your child has come to understand this principle, you may want to share with her some of the other principles involved in finance. Do not overwhelm her with too much. Start small and simple, and grow from there. Everyone progresses at their own pace. You know what works best for your child.

Chapter 10

The Importance of Friendships & Downtime

Six years as a college student has taught me that downtime and making friends are important. While I mastered a variety of technical skills at the community college, I did not build a network with other students and teachers. Being an Aspie, I never saw the importance of making friends or crafting potential work relationships. This perspective changed when I enrolled in the four-year school. The university campus offered so much more in terms of extracurricular activities and social get-togethers.

Enrolled in the electronic media program, I found myself in a crowd of like-minded people. As a result, I gained friends and acquaintances. It is important to have a major that fits your interests. Not only will you perform better on your assignments, but it will also be easier for you to build friendships.

Tips on Making Friends in College

It is a challenge for me to be tactful. When I was younger, I often ignored people who spoke to me or cut them off mid-sentence. I had to train myself with a series of simple phrases to use whenever someone spoke to me. For instance, if a person says "Hello," I say, "Hi." If an individual started a conversation with me when I was in a time jam, I said, "I'm sorry, but I need to get going. See you later." Remembering such simple phrases can change a person's outlook from "Gosh, he's a jerk" to "Oh, he's just busy. He'll get back in touch with me." People appreciate common courtesy.

Participating in lengthy conversations is another challenge. I drive my family nuts when I shared the same movie trivia over and over and over and over again, having not realized that I had done so the first three or four hundred times we saw the movie. Often, my mother said, "Hey, Jeff, you just told me this yesterday." I enjoy repetition, which extends into my conversations.

While your family understands you, most people will not. Individuals get put off when you ramble on for five minutes about the advantages of a bi-directional microphone versus an omni-directional mic. While you may find similar interests with other students in your major, they don't want to hear technical jargon. The concept of a conversation is that one person talks, and the other listens, and then the roles are reversed. This goes back and forth until the conversation concludes. Listening skills are just as important as speaking.

Paying attention to someone talking is another challenge I constantly encounter. This is more prominent when I am in the middle of a project and a person starts talking to me. It is hard for me to switch from one task to another. I often have to count to five or take a deep breath before I readjust to the new job.

However, college has taught me that listening to people does not require a whole lot of training. If you can listen to a teacher for 45 minutes on how to use a scalpel, you can certainly pay attention to a fellow acquaintance. I cannot offer you a user manual or guidebook on social interactions. The best thing you can do is join conversations. You can only learn from practice. Don't just go through the motions; concentrate on listening like you would to a professor's lecture. Details will get lost if you only partially listen and nod your head.

Other problems I have faced with social interactions is starting and keeping conversations going. I am not a fan of randomly approaching people and asking how their day is going. Rather, I have learned to find opportunities to speak with a person. In college, I learned that the best time to chat was right before class.

If a person sits next to you, introduce yourself. Here are some of the most basic conversational questions you can try.

"What major are you in?"

"How many classes are you taking this semester?"

"What year are you?"

"What are your plans after graduation?"

These are casual questions just about everyone is asked at some point in their college experience. Though simple, they make a good introduction. From there, you can decide to improve upon your relationship with that person. You might be surprised when he asks you to join him for lunch. Friendships are that easy. I met one of my best college buddies from simply asking him which classes he was taking for the semester. Our friendship grew to the point where we helped each other out on our class assignments.

College friendships tend to last much longer than friendships from high school. I say this because I've only ever kept in touch with two fellow classmates from my pre-college days. Since graduating from college, I have made several friends. I think the reason for this is because my friends and I graduated in the same major.

You will find in college that some friendships are worth pursuing while other people are just great as acquaintances. The number of acquaintances you will meet will probably outweigh the number of your friends. I define a friend as someone I can rely on in case I need her for something important like a college project, a work-related assignment, or someone to talk to about a personal issue. Acquaintances are someone you may work with on a project or carry the occasional conversation with, but not someone you would count on.

Friends are hard to come by, and it takes months, even years, to mold these relationships. I have only accumulated a half dozen people I would add to this special list. Finding someone who fits this particular category is something you can never anticipate. It just happens. When it does, it's a great thing to cherish.

Obtaining such friendships will only work if you keep true to yourself. I am aware that this sounds cheesy, but pretending to be someone that you are not is lying to both yourself and that other person. If a person you know is a sports fanatic and you hate sports, why bother to pursue a friendship with that individual? Never lie to a person over menial things like interests. The purpose of befriending someone is to enjoy his company. I would be bored to tears if I hung out with a group of guys at a football game, because that is not who I am. Knowing your interests and then finding people who share them is key.

Trust, loyalty, and reliability are also essential components in friendships. It's very easy to be sucked into a friendship where the person you view as a friend is really only taking advantage of you. With Asperger's, I often find it difficult to distinguish one from the other.

I knew one student who wanted me to access the university's equipment for a non-school-related project. I declined, but if I had gone through with this plan, I would have violated the school program's rules. I could have lost my equipment checkout privileges. You need to watch out for these types of individuals. They will claim to be your best friend if you do a small task for them, but really they just want to use you for their own personal gain. Never engage in an activity that goes against your own judgment or the school's policies.

Keep an Open Mind

Colleges are institutions for students to express themselves. They are not for the narrow-minded. With my Asperger's, I have a hard time understanding the thoughts and feelings of others. At times I say things that unintentionally come off as offensive or rude. My social ineptness has landed me in some ugly discussions.

It is good to have your own interests and perspectives on things; however, that does not give you the right to dismiss other peoples' thoughts and ideologies. I have met many individuals who are very outspoken. I rarely engaged in verbal debates, unless of course it was for a class. I never saw the point in arguing with people. The idea of college is to build friendships, not to antagonize fellow classmates. Over time, I have learned to walk away from controversial discussions on topics like religion and politics. I admit that stepping away from an issue is very difficult for me to do. Being an Aspie, I tend to cling to matters.

Even when you have many different opinions on a subject, people are still sensitive. I have found that many times people only hear what they want to hear. Sometimes, I nod my head and utter the occasional "Uh-Huh." If a person brings up a matter that you don't feel comfortable with, it's never wrong to get up and leave. You could also suggest for him to change the subject. If he refuses, then walk away. Giving a person the cold shoulder may seem rude, but it shows your disinterest in the topic and that he needs to move on to something else.

Keep in mind that colleges are places for students to exchange different views on many topics. You will hear things that you may not agree with or even find offensive. Sociology, philosophy, and religious study courses are intended for people to address sensitive issues. In participating in such discussions, you learn how to strengthen your own beliefs, possibly accept the beliefs of other students, or compromise. You are your own person.

School Organizations

University clubs are the best places to make friends and acquaintances. Depending on your college, there could be many or very few school organizations. The community college I attended only had a couple, whereas the university offered dozens. It became a habit of mine to stay on campus after class to participate in extracurricular projects as well as engage in small talk with fellow students. Being an Aspie who never really engaged in after school activities, I found this to be a different yet fun experience for me.

Participating in school organizations is usually not an academic requirement. For my major, I had to slave away for one during a whole semester, but I enjoyed working with the organization. I became one of the most enthusiastic members.

If time permits, look into attending some school organizations that fit your interests. Just know that if you join a club, you can leave if you don't like it. There is no grade involved, unlike a class. Try one out and see if it works. Make sure that it fits into your class schedule.

Dating in College

I chose not to date in college for two reasons. One, I could not fit it into my schedule. And two, I did not want to add extra stress to my already busy college life. A serious relationship can be a demanding experience. I've been in two of them, and both put a heavy, emotional toll on me.

I met plenty of attractive young ladies in college, but I only kept them as acquaintances. The ones I did find intriguing were already in relationships. "Tough luck," as my father says. In no way am I trying to dissuade you from pursuing a romantic relationship. For some people, dating is not a part of who they are. Being an Aspie, I enjoy my time alone. I never really understood the value of being in a relationship.

Before you enter a relationship, consider these questions. Are you ready to date? Do you even want to date? Plenty of people date because it's a social norm. This was not an issue for me. With my Asperger's mind, I never really felt pressured to date. And finally, ask yourself if you can manage a relationship and your studies. College is incredibly demanding. The study hours and class time add up, making free time limited and dating opportunities even more restricted.

I would approach dating like building a friendship. Although I'm furthering a male stereotype, I've noticed that many young guys pursue girls for physical reasons only. In my past relationships, I view dating as something serious, more so than just a friendship. Intimate relationships sometimes develop out of friendships. I can personally attest to this.

See where the friendship goes. Don't start a relationship with someone that you are not interested in. Begin a relationship only when you are ready. Be yourself. Do not try to wow a boy or girl by your impressive resumé or knowledge of astrology. Your particular interests might not intrigue people. They want to know what you are like as an individual.

Social Media and Communication

Technology can help you stay in contact with friends and acquaintances. You need several items to keep in touch with people, many of them Internet-based. Get a phone. For many years, I retained a flip phone that had no Internet connection or texting capabilities. You may want to make an upgrade. Look into a personal email account.

I encourage you to join a social media website like Facebook. Social media sites are very good places to keep in touch with friends, especially ones who move away or you don't get to see very often. Being an Aspie, I feel at ease with messaging and texting people rather than talking face-to-face. It has become a very acceptable form of communication in society. Be mindful of what you post online. Internet is in the public domain. Friends and potential employers can read your posts on controversial topics.

Finding Yourself Some Downtime

Both college and work will put limits on your free time. In my short life, I have learned that downtime is not so much a time to goof off as it is a state of mind. I set aside a little bit of "me time" every day. And it doesn't take too long; a simple lunch break or a five-minute mindless Internet search has provided me some mental vacations. How much you choose to set aside and what you do with that time is entirely up to you.

I have found that the best way for me to decompress was through exercise. Squeezing in a workout can be a challenge, particularly with a strict college schedule. While a ten-minute walk around campus was refreshing, pumping iron at a gym proved exhilarating.

You may want to check to see if your college has fitness facilities. Bigger state and city universities should have these available. Crunching in some workouts between classes can relieve stress from your college workload. I made it a habit to hit the gym three times a week during my college experience. If your school does not have a gym, consider looking into one outside of college. Work out when your schedule permits. If you are too busy for a gym membership, then I recommend taking long walks either around your campus or at home. I find that exercise is better than sitting in class or in front of a computer all week long. Your outlet for relieving stress may be different. Incorporate any hobby or activity that you enjoy into your daily schedule.

The one thing I would be wary about is having too much free time. I know it sounds silly, but when you are having a good time by yourself, you can forget about the clock. To help circumvent this problem, I avoided time-consuming activities. As an Aspie, once I start something, I obsess and become so engaged in the activity that I lose my sense of time. In my early teen years, I would spend hours upon hours playing video games. First-person shooter games like *Halo* and open-world ones like *Skyrim* offer so much for a gamer. Because I banned myself from video games, I could not become obsessed with them or allow them to interfere with my studies. You don't want to stay up till 2:00 AM in the morning killing space zombies or making iron daggers (like many friends I know) when you have class at 8:00 AM.

Instead, I have learned to substitute some free time activities with other ones that are less time guzzling and more productive. Working out, reading a book, or watching the latest episode of a TV show helped me accomplish the relaxation I needed without overdoing it. Self-control and moderation will go a long way for downtime. Avoiding addictive activities will help you in the long run with your education.

Note to Parents: Friendships

The only thing I have to offer for you on this topic is to allow your AS child to find his own way in making friends. In college, you cannot chaperone like in junior high or even high school. College is the time in your child's life for him to stand on his own and meet new people. Do not force him to seek friends or go on dates. If he chooses not to pursue friendships, that is his decision. Through high school, I lived in a shell like a tortoise. College was the place for me to find and build friendships. While in college, your Aspie child may discover his identity as well as make lifelong friendships.

Chapter 11

The Final Steps for Graduation

Many colleges require a capstone course in order for students to graduate. This can consist of a written thesis, a final report, or a class where students work to produce a finished product. The capstone I had to complete at the two-year school proved to be a very frustrating and stressful experience. I had to undertake a huge project. The idea behind this vast assignment was to show I had learned everything I needed to know to move into the work place.

Before I could enroll in the capstone class, I had to write a detailed proposal for the school faculty. I planned to produce a five-minute promotional video for the vocational school I attended. My proposal included a summary, release forms, a list of crewmembers, and a weekly production schedule. Before registering in this class, I spent an entire semester organizing all the materials I needed in order to proceed with my promotional video.

I felt confident and quite at ease when I submitted the proposal. I like to be prepared for a project ahead of time. *Nothing could go wrong*, I thought. One week before submissions were due, I received an email from the head of the department. He instructed me to meet with him. Sitting down before him and three other faculty members, they poked holes in my proposal, explaining what they called "inconsistencies." In short, I had to redo the whole thing in only seven days.

Ideas were tossed. New ones were created. I had to get extra crewmembers and inform the vocational school of the new updates. My schedule became hectic, but I submitted my new proposal two days before the deadline. Fortunately, I ended up enrolled in the class.

I succeeded in revising my proposal partially because friends and acquaintances came to my aid. I realized that I could not do this project alone. I had to approach my fellow classmates and ask for their help. As an Aspie, this was extremely challenging. However, I knew this needed to be done in order to succeed. In addition, to make the project more feasible, I had to reduce its size and scope. This put a lot of pressure on me, especially when I only had a week to finish.

The actual project provided one migraine after another. Students and faculty alike criticized my work, giving five-minute lectures on the most asinine things. During every class meeting, I felt like saying, "Sorry to bust your bubble, Professor So-and-So, but it's not my fault the camera is a little shaky in this shot, because the floor was unsteady to move the dolly!"

The capstone is different from other classes. It often helps prepare students for the real world. In my degree project class, teachers and students alike gave more negative feedback than in any other course. While I have developed some resistance to criticism, it became almost unbearable for me in that class. After a while, I began interpreting the feedback as personal insults. Now that I'm older, I look back at this experience and do not see it as all bad. The criticism was a drive for students to perform better on their projects.

Since I have Asperger's, I took every bit of criticism to heart. I wrote down every comment and made the proper adjustments to the video, spending hours tweaking and fixing things. Overall, this course helped me build my social skills and improve the video's quality.

My capstone at the four-year school was a bit different. Rather than having to produce my own final project, I got to choose which higher-level class I wanted to make as my capstone. I ran into some hiccups along the way. I suffered a severe injury that almost put me out of college. I will elaborate more on this story in the final chapter. After all the adventures and mishaps, I managed to graduate on time. Since my capstone involved full-time participation in a feature-length documentary, my grade was based on working within a team.

Capstone projects are stressful in nature. They are designed to make or break students. Only undergraduates who take the material seriously and do a good job make the final cut. Not all colleges require a capstone. In fact, some schools only need students to complete their core classes with a grade of C or higher to graduate.

How to Succeed with Your Capstone

Listen to the teacher's suggestions; this is the best thing you can do. During my capstone experience for my associate's degree, many students did not follow the professors' guidance. Some went as far as leaning back in their chairs while uttering the carefree "whatever." One student got into a shouting match with a teacher. Things can get ugly incredibly fast when you're showcasing your work. Going with the flow and following your professor's advice will make matters so much easier for the professor, the class, and yourself.

If possible, plan your project in advance. Start at least a month before class enrollment. Work out the proposal. Outline your thoughts and gather the materials you need. A big part of my capstone experience was managing a budget. This included writing out a proposal on how many hours and days it would take to write, film, and edit. Keep in mind that this is not far off from the time management you will have to perform in the real world.

If you are confused or have a problem, set up an appointment with one of your professors. Teachers are there to assist you. I didn't schedule a meeting for my first proposal, and it nearly cost me the class. You don't have to do it all by yourself. For my capstone, I worked with over a dozen people, including fellow classmates, teachers, and individuals outside of the classroom, to successfully complete my project. Remember, friendships can turn into work connections.

Once you are enrolled in a capstone, make sure you put all your effort into it. Either go part-time for the semester so you can devote more effort to your project or register for classes that do not require as much work. Going part-time might be a little tricky, especially if you are receiving financial aid or scholarships. Being an Aspie, I prefer to center my attention on one important assignment versus several all at once. Choosing the part-time route worked wonders for both capstone experiences. It simplified things and allowed me to focus on the capstone.

The unexpected does happen. You get sick. Your car gets a flat tire. A team member does not show up. Just about anything can occur during a capstone project. You can never be entirely prepared for the unforeseen. I ran into a situation where my audio engineer became unavailable. You may have to take some extra roles upon yourself to get the job done. I ended up being the audio engineer for the majority of my first capstone project. I had one ear in a headphone while the other listened to my interview subjects. Thank heavens for two ears! You may find yourself assuming multiple roles in your final project, though hopefully not to this extreme.

Always have a backup plan. Be flexible and do not freak out—I know it's hard for us Aspies. We like things to go according to our plans, and when they don't, we find ourselves out of our comfort zone, and who knows how we might react. If the situation proves too stressful, the best thing you can do is get up and walk away. I have learned that it is better to step back from a stressful event than let it build up inside of me to the point of a meltdown. Give yourself a few minutes to calm your thoughts. You are in control of your mind. Inform yourself that you can succeed, even when things don't go according to plan. Confidence and flexibility lead to success.

Presenting the Capstone

You may have to present your capstone before the school faculty. This can be a harrowing experience, especially if public speaking is not your strength. If you are an Aspie like me, you may have trouble speaking in front of others. Looking back, I can identify three reasons why I succeeded with my capstone presentation. First, I had taken a speech class. Second, I knew my project through and though. And finally, I had prepared my speech a week before the presentation.

Whenever you present a project in front of others, you need to take a businesslike approach. After all, a capstone reflects on you as a student. Wear nice clothes. Practice good hygiene and be well groomed. If you are a guy who sports a beard (like me), have it trimmed. I personally chose to shave for the occasion.

Make sure you speak clearly and take your time. Do not rush or talk fast. Your audience wants to hear your words with perfect clarity. If you become confused or lose a line of thought, take a deep breath and briefly refer to your notes. If you are using a projector or some other media that plays video or audio files, have it ready ahead of time. This will ensure that your presentation will go smoothly and professionally.

During the day of my capstone, the student who presented before me had not copied his files to the school computer. Right in the middle of his presentation, he bolted out of the room to retrieve them while the committee waited for him to come back. As a result of this, my presentation was shortened. I had to adapt. To this day, I do not know if he passed or failed the class. I do know that this error made his image look unprofessional in front of the school panel. Unpreparedness is an attribute both the educational and the professional world frown upon. Do not put yourself in this category.

Finally, be confident and enthusiastic. Do not talk like a robot. Having Asperger's, I find it somewhat difficult to include inflection in my voice. Try to add some energy and talk about your project in a way that shows you love it. Teachers like to see their students eager and excited about their work. If asked about problems you encountered during your capstone, mention them but do not dwell on them. Return to the positive aspects.

Steps for Graduation

Just like registering for college, there is a series of steps you need to take in order to graduate. First, meet with your academic advisor. He will go over the classes you have taken and determine whether you are ready to graduate. However, you could avoid this step by checking your degree audit. It will tell you if you have met the requirements for graduation. On my school's website, I was able to access my degree audit, and I saved it as a PDF document. After meeting all the course requirements for graduation, I needed to pay a graduation fee for my diploma.

If you plan on participating in the commencement ceremony, you will have to get your cap, gown, and honor cords (depending on your GPA). I chose not to attend my graduation. However, I was present during the ceremonial photo shoot as a photographer's assistant. I got paid to attend my own graduation—not many people can say that!

Usually at the college ceremony, you do not get your actual diploma. Instead, you receive a handshake from your school dean and a book that lists all the new graduates. It takes weeks, even months, for most colleges to deliver student diplomas. For both my degrees, it took two months before I received them in the mail. If you do not get your diploma within a couple of months, contact the college office and ask when you will receive it. The school personnel will give you a timetable for its arrival.

When some companies hire new employees, they need to see their credentials, including their educational background. Keep a copy of your degree audit. This proves you completed your education.

Notes to Parents: Being There for the Capstone

The capstone is the most demanding part of higher education. A thesis can take a toll on your AS child. Before I enrolled in the capstone for my associate's, I decided to get some filming done beforehand. The crew and I did a full day of shooting interviews. I felt confident and finished with that part of the project. In the back of my mind, I was thinking, *Perhaps I can be done with my project a few weeks ahead of everyone else.*

The first day I showed my footage to the class, I received a barrage of criticisms on technical points. The shots were either poorly lit or badly angled. Because I had started filming before the rest of the class, I felt like I was being intentionally singled out. I know that sounds ridiculous, but at the time, I did not have very thick skin. Life in general teaches you to become thick-skinned and accept criticism. For an Aspie, these are difficult lessons.

I realized I had to reshoot all that footage. This put a strain on my production schedule. The thought of re-filming everything brought on the anxiety, cannons blazing. After class that day, I felt like crying. I couldn't breathe. *All that hard work done for nothing,* I thought over and over again. I loathed my professors for being so critical. I despised the students for being so judgmental. I hated everyone! *They are all out to gang up on me!* I thought.

Before I allowed these dark feelings to take hold of me, I called my dad and told him that I needed to talk with him. When he got home from work, I shared with him the details of my first day. I discussed my paranoid feelings and what I considered to be insults. He quietly listened the whole time I spoke.

As I finished ranting, he smiled and said, "That's what college is all about."

"What?" I asked.

"To learn from your mistakes so you can do better," he explained. "Remember the schedule you planned for filming?"

"Yes," I answered. "I scheduled five days for filming."

"Well, you now have the other four to get the shots you need," he replied.

Still angry from my critique, I did not quite get his point. To settle me down, we drove to a nearby park and walked. He instructed me to talk about anything but the project.

"You need to let this go," he told me. "You can't keep it in. Clear your mind. Now it's the weekend, relax, and do what you want."

It finally sunk in how close I was to graduating. I could not let one bad review ruin my final experience at the community college. I had to persevere and learn from my mistakes. Unexpected things happen; we must resolve them and move on.

For the remaining weeks in class, I met all my deadlines. The criticism continued throughout the project, but I learned that I couldn't take the feedback personally. I also realized that no project is ever perfect. Even big production movies encounter goofs and mistakes. Ultimately I passed the class with an A. I offered some copies of my project to the vocational school, and the education board enthusiastically accepted them.

My parents have stayed with me 110% through my school, college, and work experience. Life with your AS child does not end at high school, and she will likely need your help more than you can ever anticipate as it moves along. Making an effort, even as small as a phone call once a week, can make a big difference.

I don't want to preach or say that you have to do everything for your AS child. Rather, you should act as a mentor, advising her on the right decision to make in any given situation, like a capstone project. I feel in control of my life. I greatly appreciate and thank my parents for supporting me when I needed the help.

Ask your child if you can help him. I relied on my mom a lot during the planning stage. I bounced ideas off of her on what questions to ask my interview subjects. She really offered support on the administrative end, helping me organize all the documents for my proposal.

Chapter 12

Starting Your Career

Within the first couple of months of scouring the job market, I found that my college experience did not prepare me for what lay ahead. Businesses have their own schedules, which differs drastically from education. The job hunting process is particularly frustrating and at times mind-boggling. The steps involved when seeking employment warrants its own chapter, which will follow this one. For now, I will focus on where you can begin and how to make yourself more marketable. This chapter may be helpful for all students.

When Should You Start Working?

My father started working at fourteen, and his father began at age ten. However, starting to work early does not guarantee success. As I mentioned earlier in the book, my parents instilled in me the notion that education comes first. I did not start my first job until I was 21. I worked as a student note-taker for the disability services program at the community college. My job was simple and very straightforward. I did not have to concern myself with taking orders at a drive-thru, handling customer complaints, or dealing with a whole lot of people. Since I have Asperger's, I am not a people person. I can work with others, but after a while, I get overwhelmed and it becomes too much for me.

Right out of college, I worked a couple of freelance gigs with a group of photographers. For these events, I often stood near a photographer, moving people along through waiting lines, explaining how they needed to pose and what documents they had to fill out before their pictures were to be taken. These work experiences were incredibly stressful.

Unfortunately, I discovered that many people at photo events do not listen or follow instructions. Some people yelled at me because the line was moving too slowly. The situation got worse when I had to tell some individuals to step aside when they didn't have the required paperwork. Some of these irate customers were very vocal to the point of shouting obscenities. It was very tempting for me to lash out at them, but I didn't. I learned to curb my tongue and smile through their insults.

Looking back now, I realize that these were some of the best experiences I have had as an employee. This line of work forced me out of my comfort zone, showing me that I could be more than just a technical person for video and photo shoots. On the job, you will learn new things and become more adaptable. There is no employee handbook that covers everything about a job. However, common courtesy and maintaining a professional attitude is essential to succeed in any profession.

If you are still in high school, I strongly encourage you to look for a job, even if it is unpaid volunteer work. Remember, both work and volunteer experience prior to higher education look great on a college resumé. The same goes if you are already a college student. Definitely look into volunteer work, either on campus or outside of it. A work and volunteer background also shows that you have some real-world experience. The more experiences you have had in your past, the better it will look for you as a potential employee.

College Job Opportunities and Internships

Colleges and universities alike have jobs available for students. Bookstores, learning centers, libraries, special events, and food services are only a few of the areas on campus that need positions filled. If you're looking for a little extra cash and have the time, I would take advantage of these opportunities. For one semester as a student note-taker, I received over $800.

Another thing to keep an eye out for during your college experience is internships. Depending on your major, you might be required to complete one. For my undergraduate degree, I was required to take two internships. I landed the first one at a logo design company. For that whole semester, I worked with two fellow classmates on a collection of video projects for the company's clients.

I received both an hourly pay and experience in the real world as a video editor.

There are many unpaid internships available; keep this in mind as you seek out an internship. Do not turn one down because it's unpaid. Rather, look for ones that fit into your career plan. I did two additional internships, both of which were unpaid – one was at a sound studio and the other was at a TV station. Both opened my eyes to employee expectations, business relationships, company hierarchies, and the way businesses handle clients.

It is important to realize that employers have high expectations and expect results from their employees. Seeking internships that only fit your particular talents and interests are keys to success. In college, I knew there were some topics in my major that I didn't like. I avoided internships in these areas. There were many internships available outside of those areas of study.

When you do get an internship, and if it goes well for you, talk with your supervisor. This internship may turn into a job offer upon graduation. I found that the companies I interned at did not hire the students who interned with them; however, they did offer freelance work. Never take it is an insult if the company has no positions available.

Where You Need to Begin

Building friendships in college can pay off in the long run. Networking will broaden your employment opportunities. If you develop a good friendship with someone who has graduated from your major, contact him. Ask if he has any work available. This is a good way to land a position or begin freelance work.

College professors are another resource for finding employment. Before I graduated from college, I met with one of my professors for lunch, during which we discussed the next steps in my life. This meeting gave me a confidence boost and a plan of action. When you reach your final year in college, make it a point to approach one of your teachers. Talk with him about your future career goals. Teachers in your major are great people to chat with, and they make great references.

Another resource to look into is social media sites. They are great tools for connecting with people. There are even such websites aimed at the business community. On these sites, you can post resumés and demo reels and even find job opportunities. They are also excellent for joining online groups, which enable you to learn about different local, national, or international organizations.

Upon graduation, I contacted one of my closest professors via Facebook. He added me to a college alumni group. Within the first few months of job hunting, I met with several fellow alumni for job interviews. These alumni connections made the job search process a little easier. I have learned that the people you know from college can be influential in your career search. Knowing someone in your career field makes it easier to get your foot in the door. Another option is checking out job-search sites. I have visited nearly a dozen of them, several of which have proven quite helpful. Some of the ones that I used were Indeed,

CareerBuilder, Beyond, and JobsRadar. Sites like these require logins and passwords, but most of them did not cost a penny. I would not select a site that charges fees. In my opinion, you should not have to spend money in order to get a job. There are two kinds of these sites: *1)* scams preying on the unemployed, or *2)* a legitimate service that can take weeks or even months to arrange an interview.

The same goes for job service sites. There are some reputable organizations that help people find jobs online. In fact, I used such a service to help me find a position. After a short while, though, this service proved unreliable. Within weeks of signing up, I began receiving links to job postings that did not fit my interests or skill set. Be careful. Don't put all of your energy and hopes into such a service. You need to do your own research.

Visit corporate websites and see if businesses are hiring. Many companies post job openings on their websites. Applying for a job on a company website, though, is a shot in the dark. There is no guarantee that a person will see your online application or resumé. In some instances, it took months before I got an email requesting an interview. Most of the time, I never heard back from an online application. Expect delayed responses or none at all.

The other, more old-school method of finding work is reviewing newspaper ads. You might be surprised by the kinds of jobs advertised. This is an alternative route to follow if web searching proves too daunting or slow. Don't be afraid to make calls to companies that are advertising in the paper. Talking to a person at a company is more direct and informative than wondering if your online application was even received.

With Asperger's, I found that calling numbers blindly, much less talking to people, can be challenging. I remember as a child not answering the phone when it rang because I was afraid to talk to people. It was not until my junior year of high school that I began answering the phone. I had to remind myself that phone conversations were easier to handle than face-to-face discussions. Talking on the phone does not require eye contact or physical presence.

What to Watch out for When Job Hunting

I have an unusual story to share with you. During my first month of job searching, I applied for a production assistant position at a video production company. Three weeks later, I received an email from a person claiming to be a big-shot Hollywood director. My eyes widened and my spirit lit up with glee. I had made contact with a person in the filmmaking industry! The individual asked for my address and three work references. I complied. Afterward, I began receiving instructions on how to handle some investments. I quickly realized that this was a scam.

It is very easy to fall into such a trap. If a deal sounds too good to be true, then it probably is. If a mysterious message tells you to make purchases or requests your financial account information or a social security number, ignore it. These emails fit the profile of a fraudulent scam. I would also be suspicious of a company website that requests personal information. Once you post personal data online, it is available for the whole world to view. Sites can be hacked, and your info could be at risk.

When searching for a job online, make sure you can easily access the application page without being redirected or bombarded with advertisements. I have faced this scenario several times. Rummaging through ads in order to reach a job application page is very annoying. Unfortunately, some job sites require that you fill out a survey or an ad in order to complete the application process.

If you do complete a survey, you will be exposing yourself to a world of frustration. When you begin receiving phone calls that ask if you want to further your education, then you know you've done the wrong thing by clicking or inadvertently signing up for these ad services. No application should be this irritating. Avoid the ads, and click away from the site.

If you are using a job search engine, make sure you can find the originating company website. Some company sites may require that you create a login account. These are almost always free of charge. I would do this only if you are truly interested in the job. I would be hesitant to sign up for one that requires payment. Avoid the unnecessary costs.

Keeping in Touch

Businesses receive dozens, even hundreds, of applications for a single position. They only pick a handful for a face-to-face interview and one for the job. If you do not hear back from a company within three to four weeks, then one of two things has happened. One, the job has been filled and you were not selected, or two, the business is still collecting resumés. Companies typically do not respond to all applicants.

To help settle my anxious nerves during this waiting period, I send out inquiry emails, asking the business if they have received or reviewed my applications. However, I only recommend doing this once. Businesses do not like persistent emails, they give employers the impression that you are desperate. If you do not get a reply, assume the position has been filled and move on.

If you find a company that interests you, but does not have a job listing, I suggest sending a job inquiry email to the company. The business could very well be hiring but does not have a job listing published. Only do this once. If you don't hear back, then it means the company is probably not hiring.

You must prepare a professional-looking follow-up email or letter. If you know the company's contact person, address that individual by name. If not, then address the letter with the phrase, "To Whom It May Concern." Below is a generic example I have used in many different situations over the years.

To Whom It May Concern:

My name is Jeff Kraus. I am a graduate from the electronic media program at the University of Cincinnati. At this time, I would like to inquire whether you are looking for an individual who has experience in video production, audio engineering, and/or video editing. My resumé, demo reel, and references are available upon request.

Thank you for your time.

Best Regards,
Jeff Kraus

This sample gives enough information about me and my work experiences. Companies hire because they need additional help in a particular area or department. In essence, companies consist of a group of people who solve puzzles and complete tasks for the business' best interests.

What Jobs Should You Apply For?

The above question may seem a bit broad. When you begin your job-hunting quest, you might find a variety of positions online. While applying for every job you find might seem to be a wise strategy, since it keeps your options open, this approach can be counterproductive.

When I began my job hunting journey, I applied for every position that I found. After a while, job searching became an obsession. With my Asperger's, once I start something, I get caught up in it. Some of the jobs did not particularly interest me, but in my mind, the goal was to apply for as many jobs as I could. I felt that the more jobs I applied for, the better chance I had of getting hired. I found out that is not true. Over a dozen companies turned down my applications.

Being overlooked for a position is infuriating. It annoys me even more when I don't get a response from a company. However, when applying for a position, you can only put your best foot forward. I learned not to obsess about getting an interview. The decision is beyond your control.

I strongly recommend you take some breaks from job hunting. When I was searching for work, I took every weekend off. As soon as Monday came around, I was right back at it. I treated job hunting as an occupation. I woke up, ate breakfast, and begin working to find employment.

Before you submit your application read over the job description carefully. Look for job requirements that you are comfortable with. If an occupation requires doing sales and marketing but you only know sales, then that is not a good fit for you. Sticking to your areas of expertise will help you focus on the best positions for you. I have found that it is easier to apply for fewer jobs within my skill set than a broad range.

Keep Busy

Job hunting is an opportunity for you to go out and explore new things. I recommend participating in a local group or organization. Within the first month of my career search, I had joined a writer's group. It was a nice break from the stresses of job searching. I met with people who helped me improve my writing skills.

Aside from passing the time, such activities can help you build friendships and may even help land you a job. Only join organizations or clubs that interest you. I would avoid attending groups that require payment. In my opinion, meeting new people should not cost a penny.

Getting Your Name out There

There is one more thing you can do to help make yourself more marketable, which is creating your own website. This takes work, time, and some money. However, it can pay off in the long run. The purpose behind this, if you choose to do so, is to present your work to potential employers. I highly recommend this. It is not just limited to people with technical expertise.

Unfortunately, web maintenance and updating can be time consuming. Before you decide to proceed with this idea, think hard on whether you need one. For some professions, a website is unnecessary. People in artistic fields like animation, photography, and cinematography more often have a personal website, whereas people in business or the sciences do not. Don't let your major or career path limit your decision, but only invest in a website if you think it can help you.

What you do with your site is up to you. The goal is to offer a preview of your work to future employers. I strongly suggest that you keep your site clean of technical and written errors. No one will take you seriously if you have misspellings or videos that won't load.

Finally, I also suggest designing your own business card. There are a number of reputable companies that provide this service. While this may be an old-fashioned approach, it is a good idea to have business cards available. You never know when you might meet a potential business contact.

Chapter 13

Resumé Building

Oh no! A boring chapter about writing resumés! While resumé building is not my favorite subject, it is important to learn about it. Writing a good resumé can get you an interview. Employers view candidate applications quickly and with a keen eye. Now bear with me, this chapter goes by quickly and covers a lot of ground.

The thought of sending out a resumé blindly and hoping for the best is a lazy job-hunting technique. In fact, many companies require additional items and paperwork before granting an interview, including cover letters, work references, curriculum vitae, and in some instances a portfolio. However, the resumé is the document that catches an employer's attention. I will go over what you should add on a resumé and provide additional tips. This is another chapter that applies to both Aspie and non-Aspie readers.

Keeping Your Work History Organized

One of the best courses I ever took in college was called Internship for eMedia. The class proved to be an eye-opening experience. The first assignment was to fill out a pamphlet outlining various work-related topics like past employment or production experience. After completing this, I then typed and saved that information into a file. I loaded the document with multiple headings for each particular section. It grew into what my teacher called a "resumé database."

This was an ideal project for me. As an individual with Asperger's, I love creating lists and organizing them. The purpose behind this exercise was to keep track of all my work, thus making the resumé building process easier. Having a simple document that contained my work history, education, achievements, and talents made a significant difference. With all the information organized in advance, resumé building became fast and easy.

How you organize the database is entirely up to you. Include anything and everything in your experience, even if it is as minor as volunteering at a hospital. I chose to model my resumé database from what I learned from college. Below, I have listed the type of headings used in my database.

- Work History/Internships
- Volunteer Experience
- Educational Background
- Awards & Honors
- References
- Skills & Technical Prowess

Do not send the same resumé out to every company. Most jobs you apply for will have different requirements. It is imperative to tailor your resumé to the position you are applying for. If your resumé does not list any or all the requirements for the position they want to fill, you will not receive an interview.

Formatting Your Resumé

Here's where the process becomes a bit more tedious. You need to make your resumé look good and stand out. After you create the resumé database, you must begin the process of formatting your resumé. Decide on a format and use your database to fill in the sections. Here's an example of a resumé format I used for my first job search.

Make your headers bold. Use color if necessary. You do not have to get too complicated like I did with mine. If you do not have a lot of professional or work experience, emphasize your skills, education, and any other achievements. Most employers are more interested in a person's work history and talents than his educational background. Make those sections high priority on your resumé.

You may have noticed a section called *PROFESSIONAL SUMMARY* near the top of the sample. Unfortunately, I did not learn about this section until I began my job search. The professional summary acts as an introduction. These are somewhat tricky to write. You want to impress your reader. It is kind of like a teaser to a cover letter. You give a little bit of information about yourself and how you can help the company.

The *professional summary* needs to be short and to the point. This is incredibly difficult, perhaps the most challenging part of resumé writing. Your objective is to make the reader interested in you. A professional summary is not a dumping ground to list all of your skills. It is used to sell yourself as an employee. It should be just a few sentences. What you add next is your choice. Personalize your resumé.

Resumés are usually a page long. You need to provide as much information about your skills as you can. I tend to keep the educational section the shortest. Where I went to school is not nearly as important as my skill set.

Your Name

Address: Street / City / STATE / ZIP CODE   Website:

PROFESSIONAL SUMMARY
Describe any work/employment you have participated in and emphasize how it will make you a good candidate for the job! Use vivid words! Do not just state what you have achieved!

EDUCATION

High School/College Degree
Graduation date and school

AWARDS/HONORS

(Year) Award Name
From Organization/School

SKILL/TECHNICAL PROWESS

LIST ANY SKILLS YOU HAVE ACQUIRED

WORK EXPERIENCE

Business Name [TITLE] Date (from-to)
List any tasks or assignments you've undertaken here.

Cell: E-mail:

What Not to Include in a Resumé

Do not list any hobbies or extracurricular activities you engage in. Employers probably do not care that you run track or play video games in your free time. You do not need to list an objective, even though both college and high school teachers instructed me to include one at the top of the resumé. The purpose of the objective is to state what you intend to achieve in your career. Frankly, employers are usually not interested in your goals. They are more concerned with how you can help them with their business. Unless you are enrolled in a resumé-building class, which requires you to add an objective for your grade, do not write one. Objectives are a waste of space.

I did not include references on my resumé. Many companies request references separately. Keep them in your resumé database file. Most employers do not want a personal photograph in your resumé. Some careers like acting and modeling may require them, but otherwise, only add a photo of yourself if requested.

Creating a resumé takes time, and the list of items on your resumé will grow as your career continues. I try to update my resumé database on a monthly basis. This is a good habit to get into. A couple of minutes here and there can help you bulk up your database to the point where you can't even recall every single job or skill you have acquired over the years. Save this file in a place you can access easily, specifically when you need to use it for a job search.

Writing Cover Letters

Drafting cover letters, or "CLs" as I call them, can be harder than building a resumé. Most of the jobs I have applied for requested a CL. A cover letter should not be a full-page description of yourself; rather, it should explain how your skills and experiences will help the company.

Below, I have a sample cover letter that got me my first job.

To John Smith:

I am pleased to learn that you are recruiting a content marketing assistant for your company. As a recent graduate from the electronic media program at the University of Cincinnati, I have acquired a vast range of skills that apply to both visual and written mediums.

Through my undergraduate program, I have honed qualifications that are directly related to your needs:

- Creative and technical writing skills
- Research and social web competencies
- Basic HTML coding
- Microsoft Word, Excel, & PowerPoint fluency
- Photo, video, and graphic design experience

Writing is a passion of mine. I am a published author of the award-winning book The Aspie Teen's Survival Guide. Organizing that book has opened my eyes to the often tedious and meticulous process of writing. Catching a target audience with appropriate and descriptive language is essential, especially in the fields of marketing and public relations. My book has given me such a wonderful experience. As a college student, I worked as both a copywriter and a photographer for the University of Cincinnati organization Bearcast Media. This experience has taught me that the Internet community demands quality and easily accessible content. Freelancing as a SEO writer has shown me the need to utilize important phrases and words to capture a reader's attention. I am the type of individual who enjoys working on both independent projects as well as in groups. I work fast, am accustomed to strict deadlines, and have a knack for close attention to detail.

I welcome the opportunity to discuss how my skill set and strengths can help your company.

Sincerely,

Jeff Kraus

I listed the position for which I was applying in the letter. This position happened to be a content marketing assistant. I explained my qualifications for the position, shared my work and college experiences, and explained how these experiences molded me into a good applicant for the position. Incorporating your past work and personal experiences can work to your advantage.

Curriculum Vitae

A curriculum vitae, or a CV, is like a cover letter and a resumé combined, but is much more detailed. These are rarely required for a job application. I had applied for two positions at educational institutions, both of which required this document. For a CV, you prepare a detailed listing from your resumé database. It needs to be attractive and precise.

The purpose of a CV is to give an employer a more in-depth view of your history. Resumés are only a page long, whereas a CV can be several pages. The length will depend on how much information you have in your resumé database. If you are older like me, it will be longer than someone who has just graduated from high school.

I arranged my curriculum vitae as follows:

- Experience/Volunteer Work
- Employment History
- Educational Background
- Skills
- Awards and Honors
- Interests

You might wonder why the last item is on the list. Though not required, your interests give an employer insight into your personality. As mentioned previously, with my Asperger's, I can only talk to people on a casual basis, but I would make a terrible customer service representative. I prefer working in a peaceful, secluded environment. I won't burden you with a sample of my CV, as that would add too many pages to this book.

Work References and Recommendation Letters

References or letters of recommendation are required by most job applications. Letters of recommendation provide a look at your work skills and experiences from an unbiased third-person perspective. Building strong, positive relationships with faculty members will provide you resources for such recommendations when applying for employment.

Before you begin your job hunt, contact individuals who impacted your college life. Ask them if they would write a recommendation letter for you. Do not be disheartened if a person turns you down. Simply move on and find someone else. Once you have gathered a couple of letters of recommendation, keep them in a safe place. I advise scanning them into a computer. This way, you can email copies or simply print them off.

When you list a reference, include that person's name, job title, email, and phone number. These are the bits of information employers need in order to verify your references. Contact your references if you need to retrieve their information.

One Last Footnote

When you apply for a position at a company, ask their policy on retaining resumés. On average, businesses hold onto them for 30 days, and then they are discarded. This means you may want to reapply after that time.

Chapter 14

The
Interview

For a young Aspie with little to no work experience, the mere notion of a face-to-face job interview can be unnerving. The idea of sitting in a large corporate office with a group of people who ask you about your qualifications can be overwhelming. Take a breath. Job interviews can actually be very relaxed and interpersonal. Keep in mind that the interview is a tool used by employers to select or weed out applicants. Just because you get the interview does not mean you will get the job.

Attending the Interview

When you get an interview, a company representative will set a meeting date and time. If you are unavailable on the appointment date, reply to them in the same manner they contacted you. When you do this, you run the risk of not receiving an interview.

Once the appointment is set, you need to find directions to the interview location.

I recommend that you take a test drive to the location of the interview. This is very helpful if the meeting is in an unfamiliar part of town. It is stressful enough to prepare for the interview. You do not want the added anxieties of battling traffic and locating where you need to go.

Look Your Best!

The saying that the first impression is the last impression rings true in the business world. If you show up to a job interview with disheveled hair, bad breath, a T-shirt, and shorts, your appearance tells the employer that you won't take the job seriously. As an individual with Asperger's, maintaining personal hygiene is somewhat of a challenge. I have difficulty comprehending other peoples' outlooks and perspectives, and I don't always take care of my appearance.

Since my childhood, my parents drilled into me the morning procedure of preparing for school: eating breakfast, bathing, brushing my teeth, and dressing in a new set of clothes. I learned that these mundane activities were just as essential as showing up on time for school or work. You don't have to look like a movie star or a model, but you should look well groomed. Shower, brush your teeth, use deodorant, and comb your hair. These simple steps make you look presentable.

Now, you might ask, how should I dress for the interview? It depends on the company you are interviewing with. I prefer to overdress for the first interview. I recommend wearing khakis or slacks with a buttoned shirt, and no gym shoes. With a professional practice like law and accounting, I suggest you wear a suit and tie. Keep your shirt tucked in and your belt tight, and avoid sagging pants at all costs.

While you may not notice it, people pick up on sloppy appearances and bad hygiene. My father had a certain knack for knowing when I had not brushed my teeth. As a pubescent teenager, my father would wave his hand in front of his face whenever I spoke.

"Jeez, Jeff, your breath stinks," he would say. "Did you forget to brush your teeth again?"

Of course he was mostly exaggerating. The point, though, was to point out my horrible breath. You may want to consider chewing a breath mint.

For young ladies with autism-related disorders, I suggest wearing skirts and blouses. You may want to look into women's suits as an alternative. Do not break the bank for a new outfit, though. Modest makeup is okay, but don't overdo it.

Keep your personal items to a minimum. You do not need to bring a purse, or as my father calls "a suitcase" to an interview. It gives employers the impression that you are not organized enough to house your own belongings. Use a wallet or a small pouch to keep your items safe. The same goes for guys. The only things you should carry when walking into an interview (aside from car keys and wallet) is a copy of your resumé, a cover letter, a notepad and pen for notes, and, if requested, your portfolio.

Pre-Interview Advice

It is a good idea to organize a list of questions before the interview. While the employer will ask you questions, you should also make some inquiries of them. Below are some sample questions I used during some of my job interviews.

- What are the hours and work schedule for the job?
- What is the work environment like? Will I be in an office or a cubicle?
- Will I be working alone or within a team?
- What type of projects/assignments does the job involve?
- How long has the company been in business?
- What is the longevity of supervisors and management?
- Is there opportunity to grow in the company?
- What is the dress code?
- What are the benefits? Health insurance? Dental? Vision? 401(k)?
- Is the pay hourly or salary based?

You do not have to use all of these questions. These are just some samples you might use. I advise against asking too many questions about compensation. If you start asking about the compensation amount, this tells the hiring manager that money is your primary motivator. This will backfire on you. Money should only be talked about during the hiring stage, which I'll cover in the next chapter.

Have your questions ready before you start the interview. Not only will it show the employer your interest in the position, but also the company. Planning everything out makes things less stressful; living under my parents' roof has taught me that. Heaven thank them for instilling those skills in me at a young age!

It is wise to research the company before you meet for the interview. Reviews and input on social media sites can help you gauge what the company is like. In truth, you will not become familiar with the work environment until you are employed. As a side note, if you search for the company online and do not find a website or any social media presence, I would be a little suspicious. This is a good reason to do your own research.

When commuting to the company's location, make sure to give yourself enough time to arrive a couple of minutes early. It is always good to be punctual, but it is better to be there slightly ahead of time. Doing so tells the employer that you care enough about the job to arrive a few minutes early. Arriving early also gives you the chance to help settle your nerves.

As an Aspie, I also get very anxious. The stress of missing or being delayed for my appointment vanishes when I arrive a couple of minutes ahead of time. I have the chance to organize my thoughts and questions. In my experience, these few minutes before the interview have helped me greatly.

Coming early to an interview, though, does not mean arriving 30 minutes before it begins. Doing this will tell the employer that you have no regard for them or their schedule. You would also probably find yourself sitting in the lobby for a long time, which is never a fun thing (I have been there, and it sucks).

Interview Etiquette

During my internship class at the community college, I learned the many skills I would need to navigate an interview, including speech, posture, and mannerisms. Job interviews are actually quite simple and straightforward. One or several people might interview you. Four people interviewed me for my second internship. It is unnerving to be examined by four sets of eyes.

Sit up straight in your chair. An upright posture shows confidence. Keep your hands in your lap. If your palms sweat or hands shake, then sit on them. This may sound silly, but taking your hands out of the equation can resolve some of that nervous twitching.

Since my early childhood years, I always bounced my knee when I got anxious. It drove my mother nuts whenever I began twitching my leg. When we sat at the dinner table, she often swatted it like an annoying fly. Nervous tics draw people's attention. During my job interviews, I tried not to shake my leg.

I am aware that fidgeting is a method some people, especially individuals with Asperger's, use in order to keep themselves calm. It shifts all that nervous energy into one repetitive, physical activity. However, this kind of activity does not present you well to a potential employer. It is understandable to be a little anxious, but you do not have to show it.

Whenever I arrived a few minutes before an interview, I used that time to manage my anxiety. I took deep breaths and thought positively. I knew I could do well. I've had some very good yoga teachers. From them, I learned how to maintain my composure in stressful situations. Deep breathing techniques and a confident outlook could make your job interview experience less harrowing.

Ask your parents if you can do a mock interview. I did this on multiple occasions with my family. My mother pointed out my mistakes and helped me improve my interview skills. Keeping eye contact is important for a job interview. Employers (rather people in general) expect eye contact. They will consider it rude if you don't make eye contact.

As an adult with Asperger's, I had to train myself to look people in the eye. I prefer to have multiple people interview me, because I can look from person to person. This might not be the case for your interview. You can cheat by focusing on the person's nose or mouth. This has helped me.

Remain confident and take your time when talking. If you do not understand a question, ask the person to repeat it. The type of questions the employer may ask will vary. Some are quite direct, while others are more open-ended and ambiguous.

One hiring manager asked, "What is your dream job, and how does it apply to our company?" This was the toughest question I was ever asked. Before blurting out a response, I had to think very hard. I ended up telling him that since the job involved video production, I was looking forward to growing within a production house as an editor and producer.

You must be candid with your answers. While your skills may qualify for the position, the employer wants to take into account how you will fit into the job and the work environment. Often times, this can cause you not to get hired. There is no point in being part of a company that you do not find interesting or has a working environment that does not fit your personality. The following are some sample questions you might be asked:

- Tell me a little bit about yourself.
- What is your work history?
- Where did you go to college? What was your major?
- Where do you see yourself five years from now?
- Why did you choose our company?
- What skills do you have that may benefit our company?
- Do you prefer to work alone or with others?
- If you were an animal, what animal would you be? (Yes, I have been asked that before.)

Toward the end of the interview, the employer will often ask if you have any questions. This is your opportunity to learn more about the company. I always brought a notepad and pen for this very reason. Write down their answers if it will help you. Job interviews vary in length. Some are as short as 15 minutes, while others may take over two hours. I have found that the shorter interviews are more formal, whereas the longer ones are more conversational. Of the two, I prefer the latter. When an interview was carried out in a casual, easygoing way, it lessened my anxiety.

For my second internship, the interview lasted two hours. Most of the time, the employers played my demo reel on a computer screen and asked me questions about each project. The interviewers handled the meeting in a very laid-back, relatively stress-free manner. I ended up having a great time chatting with them.

When the interview ends, shake hands with the interviewer and thank him for his time. Ask how long this process may take and when you might hear from them. Then, continue your job search. Don't place all hope in one potential position.

From my experience, the first couple of interviews were a bit intense. I was not entirely sure how to handle myself, but with each interview, I felt a little more relaxed. I began to understand how they generally go. The anxiety will always be there. Be honest, remain confident, and show courtesy. Most importantly, know what the employers want and explain how you can be a benefit for their company. When your interview concludes, you should walk away feeling self-assured. I have never left an interview feeling embarrassed or defeated. Consider the interview an accomplishment.

Notes for Parents: Helping with the Interview

This is your child's interview. He is in the lead. You can still help him in more subtle ways. You might want to consider assisting him with the interview questions. Try engaging in a mock interview with him. My parents also helped me with fashion. Learning to put on a tie with my father's help was an interesting experience. When it came to tying the knot, I even confused him.

Preparing for the first job is a rite of passage. For fathers with AS sons, I suggest going over the necessary fashion tips for a job interview. If your child has challenges with buttoning shirts or tying ties, show him these processes. An activity like this can give you some quality moments with your son. For mothers with AS daughters, I encourage you to go over fashion and personal grooming. Being a dude, I'm not a specialist on women's wear—I leave that entirely to you. Reviewing makeup and selecting clothing will help your AS daughter. It will also enhance your mother-daughter relationship.

Chapter 15

Sealing the Deal

I received two employment offers on the same day. My elation from these proposals turned quickly to anxiety. Which job would I be better suited for? Which one would be more beneficial to my career? Should I select one out of convenience? My thoughts swirled into a vortex. There were two offers on the table. How could I choose the right one?

I spoke with my parents before I made a decision. We talked about which job would be a better fit for me. I also spoke with other family members and several close friends. This was an important decision. I took my time to choose for myself. I accepted one of the positions by the end of the week.

How to Choose a Job

When employers find a viable candidate, they want to hire him quickly. In doing so, the company offers you a compensation package, which includes wages and benefits. For your first job, you may not have a lot of room to negotiate your compensation. Money should not be the only factor in your final decision. There are many other factors that fit into the equation, such as work hours, vacation time, the company's location, and the work environment.

Questions that you may not have covered during the job interview can be answered during this phase. Before I chose either job, I wrote out a series of additional questions I had not asked during the interviews. Below are some extra inquiries you may want to consider.

- What are the policies for vacation and sick time?
- What is the pay schedule?
- Is there direct deposit for paychecks?
- What other benefits are there, such as disability, healthcare, eye care, or 401(k)? How long before I am eligible to receive them?
- What are the payroll deductions for my benefits?
- Is there employee parking?
- How much time is allotted for lunch?

Send out your inquiries sooner rather than later. Doing so reinforces your interest in the position. The hiring personnel will often respond quickly. The employer may set a date for you to make your decision. A shorter timeframe can add more stress. People who seem pushy or even demanding come off as antagonizing in an Asperger's mind. However, it is a good thing when an employer is a bit eager to hire you, as she sees you as the best candidate.

It is important to consider how the job will fit into your career plan. Quite literally, this is your show. You cannot and should not have someone else make the decision for you. Weigh your options, talk them over with your friends and family, and then make your decision. Do not dawdle or leave the employer hanging in suspense. Delaying your decision may depict you as a person who can't make up his mind.

Sealing the Deal

The day I accepted my first full-time job, I called my future employer and told him that I wanted the position. The conversation lasted two minutes and was mostly composed of phrases like "Jeff, welcome aboard," and "Thank you so much, sir." Despite the short conversation, making that phone call was one of the smartest things I ever did in my young career. Under certain circumstances, people want to hear a "yes" or "no" answer. Making a phone call shows your interest in the job.

You might start working the following week, or even the next day. Enjoy your remaining free time! The human resource staff will provide with the forms you need to complete. I won't bore you with details, just know there will be paperwork and that it is mandatory for you to complete it in a timely manner. Fill out the paperwork honestly and write legibly. If there is a section you do not understand, make note of it and ask your employer about it. Insurance documents are often written in a way that only insurance or business employees can understand.

Never complete a document without fully reading and understanding it. If you do not feel comfortable asking the HR department for clarification on your inquiries, look for some outside advice from your parents. For my first new job, I spent a good part of an evening going over the insurance plans with my father. We gathered a collection of questions about the documents. I then proceeded to ask them at a later date.

Starting the New Job

My first day at work was slow and quite uneasy. I was in an unfamiliar environment. I didn't know the people or what they expected from me. It was like the first day of school. I dressed like I had for the job interview—khakis, nice shoes, and a buttoned shirt. I was the most overdressed employee in the office. I sat at a desk for eight hours, growing more and more uncomfortable. The shoes I wore hurt my feet. All day they had been resting on a hard tile floor. Cramps fired up my calves and knees. I felt like I was developing workout pains, even though I had not been exercising. When I finished my first day, I literally had to shuffle to get to my car. I also started developing the weirdest sensations throughout my body. My chest began shaking, and my legs grew cold. I wondered if I had caught the flu.

I talked with my mother to help settle my mind. I told her everything about my day, the good and the bad. I spoke for fifteen minutes non-stop. When I had finished, she told me that I was just anxious.

I was facing a new phase in life. Transition for people with Asperger's is difficult. We need stability and consistency. In my situation, I was unaccustomed to the new environment, the duties of the job, the people, and sitting at a desk for hours on end. This was a much different experience from high school or college. My mother was right.

I knew deep down I had nothing to fear. The job surrounded me with good people and a relatively tame environment. The anxiety held its grip until I fell asleep that night. The following day proved a better experience. I dressed in casual, comfortable clothing. I packed a water bottle and walked laps around the building during my breaks. From then on, things moved a bit more smoothly.

It is normal to feel nervous during your first few days at a new job. You learn what works and what does not. As one of my greatest college professors said to me on several occasions, "Work is very much on the fly." Projects arise and fall. You will work on one and be drawn to another at a moment's notice. Note to Aspies: you don't need to freak out at your first job. I survived without having a meltdown.

A full-time job often provides a repetitive schedule. You wake up, eat breakfast, dress, commute to work, put in 8 to 10 hours, and return home. The next morning arrives, and you begin again. Being an Aspie, I love a structured routine. Living in the moment or making things up as I go drives me crazy. There will be times when you have to solve problems or troubleshoot an issue very quickly. I have had projects pop up on me at the last minute. However, these are exceptions. You may hate getting up between six or seven in the morning. After a week's time, it will become part of your daily routine.

On my third day at my first job, I awoke at 5:35 AM, feeling rested and ready to go. I know that sounds absurd! However, it doesn't take long to readjust your sleep cycle. It may differ for you, especially if you like sleeping in until noon. In that case, you will have to make an effort to get up early. Turn on that screeching alarm clock!

Blending In

As an individual with Asperger's, I cannot easily adapt or readjust to a new environment. Understanding other people's feelings, comprehending sarcasm, and even understanding humor is a challenge. Much of the world does not understand Asperger's or autism-related disorders. While I have stressed the need for you to be yourself in earlier chapters, there are limitations in the work environment.

Most nine-to-five jobs require a little bit of conformity. You walk in on time, say "Hello" to your fellow co-workers, sit down at your workspace, and begin working. The urges for engaging in repetitive rituals or isolating yourself from others are not acceptable in the workplace. At some point, you will have to work and communicate with others. Certain phrases and keeping eye contact (or the cheat tip I gave you about eyeballing people's noses) can help you endure these awkward situations.

Always greet your colleagues. A simple "Hello" or "How are you doing?" will suffice. Conversations never need to be long, especially when you are starting out in the morning. It takes me awhile to form bonds with new people. Surprisingly, I find myself drawn toward extroverted individuals who constantly smile and uphold a cheerful attitude. As for quieter folks, like myself, it takes a little more time for me to befriend them. Kind of weird, isn't it?

Exposing yourself to social situations will help you understand your colleagues' personalities. Over the years, I have grown a child-like interest in comprehending people's feelings. For a long time, I equated a loud voice to yelling, whereas I associated a quieter voice to shyness. As a young adult, I discovered this logic was not sound. Some people naturally talk loud, while others are soft spoken. Listening to the way people speak and how they phrase their words can help you understand their feelings. There is no guidebook for this skill. Mine is still extremely limited. People who speak in a monotone or a dry voice make it hard for me to fully "get" their feelings.

A few years back, I worked with a guy who always spoke in a monotone voice. He also said things that I interpreted as offensive and mean spirited. It got so bad that I told him I was done working with him. Before I left, he approached me and explained he was only kidding. He did not intend to hurt my feelings. His reconciliation changed my perception of him.

This sort of miscommunication can lead to many problems. If a colleague says something you do not understand or find hurtful, address it with that individual. I have found that colleagues do not intentionally irritate one another.

Additional Advice for the First Job

Before you head out the door, I suggest you organize all of your items ahead of time. Searching for a misplaced phone is one of the worst ways to start off the morning. How my morning goes often determines my mood for the rest of the day. I always set my belongings in the same place. If permitted, I recommend that you take a water bottle to work. You will be sitting a lot if your job is in an office environment. Every hour, if possible, get up and stretch your legs. Taking bathroom breaks and filling up water bottles are perfect reasons to move around. For my first full-time job, I was given a 30-minute lunch window and two 10-minute breaks. I divided those breaks over the course of each day. Being a person who can't sit still for too long, I always find an opportunity to stand and move around.

I have started visiting the gym after work. Though my mind may be tired, my body craves activity. Squeeze in some workouts if you can. Being active can help you develop a more positive perspective.

Enlightening Facts about the First Job

Your first job is not going to be the only one in your career. There are opportunities to grow in the company or to move on to other employers. Simply put, it is your first job. Look at it as the initial stepping stone in a long path of your career. To an Asperger's mind, this is especially hard, given our lack of transitioning skills and desire for certainty. I'm only starting out in the work world. I have no idea what will happen in my future.

There are so many possibilities for you. As my mother told me on many occasions, "You can't live life like an ostrich." Opportunities in life fly along like sheets of paper on a windy day. You have to reach out and grab them. If you are not looking, you will miss them. Also, you have to focus on the task in front of you.

There are some downers that come with the first job. The following facts may not apply to all entry-level positions. One, the pay is not the greatest. Two, it may take months before you can be eligible for the company's healthcare plan. And three, vacation time and sick days are not offered in the first year.

It takes months, even up to a year before you can fully adjust to the new work environment. Where I work, I still see myself as the "new guy," especially since I'm one of the youngest employees. My intent is not to stress you out, but to give you fair warning. Ask for guidance when you need help and keep a notepad or notebook available to jot down some important notes. Post-it notes and notepads have also been very helpful in my young career.

Downtime from Work

Do not bring your work home with you. Unless otherwise stated by your supervisor, I encourage you to adopt this strategy. When outside of the workplace, you need time for yourself and your family.

There is more to life than working and being alone. Go out and do things. Exercise, participate in social gatherings, or work on an art project. Do whatever fun and creative activities you enjoy. As my father always told me when I was young, "You are part of the world." Just because you have an autism-related disorder, doesn't mean you have to live a solitary life.

Note to Parents: Helping with the Transition into the Work World

This is a new chapter in your AS child's life. When she receives a job offer, be present as a guide instead of a manager. The job your child chooses to accept is her decision. The first job is a big step into the real world. She will learn what her strengths and weaknesses are through her work experiences. Be there to offer advice and answer any questions.

The day I got my first job, my father and I bonded over a beer and pizza. This was nothing particularly special, but it gave us a few hours to talk about my thoughts and feelings. It also provided my father an opportunity to share his own experiences at the start of his career. Doing something like this might be worth considering. Food and talk go well together.

Chapter 16

The Many Facts about Traveling

During my senior year of college, I took two long-distance trips from my home state of Ohio. One was to Europe and the other was to northern California. Both of these journeys exposed this Aspie to the important ins and outs of traveling. Though you may not imagine yourself going to other parts of the world anytime soon, traveling is still an important topic worth addressing.

I will share some tips on how to prepare for long-distance travel, including the basics like how to pack, get a plane ticket, and so on. These tips pretty much apply to any reader. I will also present ways for people with Asperger's to cope with the stresses of traveling. I warn you, traveling on your own, especially for people with autism-related disorders, is an out-of-your-element experience.

What to Pack

Packing for travel is a skill we learn. Unfortunately, I did not acquire this skill until I was a teenager. Since I have Asperger's, I have difficulty organizing a multi-step project. A short trip like driving to work and back is easy, whereas planning a trip that requires an airline flight, packing, and a hotel is hard to handle. I am often clueless as to what to pack for a weeklong trip.

If you run into this issue, here's some helpful advice. Not only does it matter what you pack, but also how you pack. Before you stuff your luggage with clothing and toiletries, you have to think about what you actually need for the trip. For one, you need something to wear. You need to know the weather conditions of where you're going before you begin packing. The World Weather Information Service's website is a good place to catch up on climate in any part of the world. Once you know the weather, pack accordingly.

Rather than immediately cramming your suitcase with personal belongings, hoping that it will close, I recommend laying out all your items. Aside from making the packing process a bit more organized, this practice will help you identify all your effects. If it helps, I suggest creating a typed or written checklist of what you need. I did this for my trip to Europe.

This idea sounds a bit intense, but it is an extra step that really helps. It gives you an early opportunity to review and perhaps change your list of items. By doing this, it gave me peace of mind. There may be some things you will forget to pack but you can always purchase them at your destination. I suggest you begin packing several days before the trip.

What you take on your trip is up to you. Some of the items will depend on the type of trip. For instance, if the trip is work-related, you will probably need a briefcase, a computer, and work-related clothing. If it is a vacation in the Caribbean, you will pack a much different wardrobe.

To keep your trip simple, I suggest bringing only the essentials. How much you pack depends on the length of the trip. Remember, you have to carry the luggage. Below are the basics you will need:

- Several sets of clothing (shorts, pants, and shirts)
- Socks and underwear
- A small case for any medications
- An extra pair of glasses (if you wear them)
- A pouch housing all your personal hygiene items
- Other sundries

If you are bringing something you need immediate access to, like medications or a laptop, I would recommend putting them in a carry-on. A backpack is a good carry-on to bring on a plane. They are not very big, and you can wear them.

What Not to Pack

There are many things you should not pack. Food and water are not permitted on air flights. On several occasions, flight attendants have singled me out for carrying a water bottle in the boarding line. Each time I had to toss the bottle away, even if it was half full. These are the air travel regulations.

I would not pack valuable items in my luggage. You should carry expensive items like jewelry and electronics on your person or in your carry-on. You do not want them in your luggage. It is very easy for valuable belongings to be damaged or even lost.

How to Pack

By design, luggage is meant to limit what items you bring. With Asperger's, I find this aggravating. As a child, I loathed traveling for this very reason. *I should be able to take whatever I want. How can I fit everything into a single case?* When I packed, I frequently crammed as much as I could into my suitcase, praying that it would stay shut.

As an adult, I know to pack only what I need. After I gather all the items I need to bring with me, I begin folding my clothes length wise in thirds and then roll them up nice and tight into little cloth cylinders. Folding and rolling clothing shrinks their size down significantly. As a result, you can pack a lot more into your suitcase. This packing technique has helped me greatly. When I see that my suitcase is only partially full with the clothing I need, I feel a sense of relief. I don't feel as anxious over the idea that I won't be able to fit everything I need for the trip.

As an extra packing tip, I suggest you only keep clothing and personal hygiene items in your checked luggage. If it gets lost, you are only missing shirts, pants, and a toothbrush. In the carry-on bag, pack everything else, including a day's worth of clothing. This technique has saved me in the past. During a trip to Berlin, one of my connecting flights ran late, eating into my layover time. I literally had to run in order to catch my flight. Though I managed to board the plane, my luggage was not so fortunate. For two days, I had to live off of the clothes on my back and the content of my carry-on.

Make your carry-on your backup plan. Depending on how far you travel, the carry-on can make the difference between an enjoyable or miserable trip. Make sure your carry-on is not very large. Airports are very strict about the size of carry-on baggage. If you have sensitive materials in your carry-on, make sure they are protected.

Getting Plane Tickets

Do research on available flights from different airlines. You can check out the airline's website to get your tickets. If the airline reservation service is confusing, you might want to get in touch with a travel agent. I took this approach for my trip to Germany. Relying on an experienced travel agent can relieve some stress. They understand all the little details of traveling, like which airport is better to fly from and which ones offer the best connecting flights. If you do not travel a whole lot and are planning to make a long journey, particularly between different countries, this would be a wise choice.

As a first-time international traveler, it was important for me to have my air travel planned well in advance. I made my plane reservations to Germany several months in advance. By doing this, I had an excellent choice of seating. I did not have to worry about being put on standby. Plane tickets disappear quickly. The sooner you get your tickets, the better.

If you can afford it, I recommend booking a first-class ticket. While this will be more expensive than flying coach, it has many benefits. You are in a separate seating area from other passengers. This makes the in-flight journey more tolerable, especially the separation from loud children. With Asperger's, my hearing is very sensitive. I find the cries of a small child piercing and agonizing. If you have sensitive hearing, first class is a viable option. It is generally a smaller area and less crowded, which is great if crowds are not your thing.

You get better food and service in first class. On a short flight, this may not make much difference, but on a long one, it improves your experience. First-class gives you more individualized service than coach. The seats are bigger and much more comfortable, and you can recline and stretch your back. This is great flexibility to have, especially for those eight-hour or longer flights.

At the Airport

Airlines have a rule that, once you buy a ticket, you can only print a boarding pass within a short time before the actual flight. For international flights, you can only get boarding passes at the airport. Having your ticket in advance will help release some of that extra anxiety. The fewer things you need to do at an airport, the better.

If you have to use a kiosk for your boarding pass, you need to identify yourself. If you have trouble with the kiosk, approach one of the airport employees. Generally, there are at least a couple service staff members standing near flight check-in to help people with the kiosks and their baggage. These individuals will show you how to use the kiosk. It is crucial to have your ticket in hand before you check in. You need your boarding pass before you go through security. I know it is frustrating to wait until the last moment to get your boarding pass. I prefer to have everything organized and ready well in advance as much as possible (unfortunately, some things happen at the last minute).

Once you get your boarding pass and check in your luggage, you have to go through security. Following an assembly line of people never sat well with me. Aside from disliking large crowds, I prefer to move at my own pace. Passengers in line tend to become frustrated very easily; they do not like it when individuals move slowly. A guy once cut in front of me because I had trouble untying my shoes. I lost my spot and had to catch up with the rest of my belongings, which had already moved through the security checkpoint.

To avoid feeling rushed at the security checkpoint, I always have my ID and boarding pass in hand before entering the line. Being ready makes it easier for you, the other people in line, and the security personnel. Follow the security personnel's instructions and be cooperative. If necessary, step aside to make sure all your belongings are ready for inspection. Allowing others to move ahead of you is better than hurrying through the checkpoint and making mistakes along the way.

Do not panic if you set off the alarm as you walk through the scanning booth. This has happened to me on a couple of occasions.

Step back and wait for instructions from the security personnel. Check for any loose items that you could be carrying. I have learned to do what I call the "idiot check," which is to confirm twice that I have not misplaced any items.

Simple Tips for Overseas Traveling

When traveling overseas, you may find yourself in a very unfamiliar environment. People speak a language you may not understand. The signs do not make any sense. The currency is different. Your internal clock is off by several hours. These and many other issues come with traveling abroad. Overseas traveling deserves its own section in this book, because there are so many details to cover.

Before I begin, there is a matter I need to address. Overseas traveling can be very dangerous. Unsuspecting travelers can fall victim to a number of criminal elements. Other dangers come with traveling: chances of getting lost, misplacing your passport, or even contracting an illness you have not been vaccinated for.

On the flip side, traveling abroad can also be a fun and enjoyable experience if you think and act smartly. If you're planning your first trip overseas, I strongly recommend that you find a flight companion. When I traveled to Germany on a class trip, a classmate shared the same flights with me. This turned out to be very handy. When our luggage did not arrive at our final destination, we worked together to locate baggage claim. Having a flight partner can also make the long flight time easier to endure.

Even though I have Asperger's, I still find the presence of other people comforting, especially in an unfamiliar environment. If I had flown without a flight buddy, the anxiety and over-stimulation that is associated with my AS could have been much more difficult for me. This is why a flight partner is important. Even if you do not know what to do or where to go, you at least have another person with you in the same situation. Two working together is better than one.

You must be mindful of your surroundings. Keep your head up and scan the surrounding area. Pay attention to the entrances, exits, and the people nearby. I am aware that people watching is hard for us Aspies. I still have difficulty making eye contact with strangers, but observing other people does not require eye contact. Look around and identify the people near you—their clothing, hairstyle, and features. This can be a very good practice on which individuals to avoid or approach. I will go over this in greater detail in the next chapter.

Paying attention to your surroundings helps if you get lost. Signs are important, especially in a foreign airport. They will become your guide for navigating through the airport. Remember, flight attendants and people who work at the airport are very good individuals to approach if you have questions.

Before I ask for help from an airport employee, I think hard about what I am going to ask. I formulate the question in my head. By the time I approach the employee, I have the question memorized so I can ask it without fumbling my words or losing my train of thought. I keep my eyes on the person's face or an item near him to create that illusion of making eye contact. I listen carefully to the answer and then ask questions to clarify any misunderstandings.

What You Need for Overseas Traveling

The materials you will need for a foreign trip are few but essential. Foremost, you must have a passport. Make sure you sign it before you leave your home. For my flight to Amsterdam, an attendant yelled at me because I had not signed my passport. An unsigned passport is almost as bad as not having one. Your signature is proof that your passport belongs to you. I got lucky when I borrowed a pen from a man who did not speak English.

If you misplace your passport during your journey, you run the risk of getting stuck in the country. If this happens, your only option is to go to your nation's embassy. This is a predicament I have fortunately not encountered. Having a copy of your embassy's phone number can come in handy.

The next items you need are a Photo ID and a driver's license. Like the passport, these items can be used as identification. Keep those items with you at all times. Have a health insurance card. This can help you out of a bind in case you get injured or sick.

When you arrive at your final destination, buy a phone that will work in that region; this is crucial in case of an emergency. A cell phone from your home country may not work. Airports have stores that sell electronics.

You also need to have some of the country's currency. Contact your bank to find out the conversion rate (this fluctuates every day).

How much money you convert for your trip is entirely up to you. I cannot say for certainty about other parts of the world, but Europe is quite pricy. It is better to have more cash than you need than to not have enough. When you come back from your trip, you can always convert your leftover foreign currency. You are usually charged fees to convert currency.

To summarize, you need a passport, a photo ID, a driver's license, a health insurance card, a workable phone, and local currency. I recommend keeping all these items housed in a handy, portable container, like a fanny pack. Male Aspies may think fanny packs are only for old ladies; well, they are not. Wearing one and keeping it secure will ensure that you won't misplace any important documents. When you take the pack off at your hotel, place it in your room's safe, or hide it in a place that you will not forget.

Flights and the Frustrations of Delays

For you frequent flyers or occasional air travelers, you have probably faced the frustration of a delayed or canceled flight. As an Aspie, delays and cancellations drive me nuts. I expect everything to go according to plan and on schedule. Any changes in plans or delays raise my stress level significantly. I find unplanned events hard to live with.

I had two layovers when I flew to Germany. One was in Atlanta and the other was in Amsterdam. In Atlanta, the pilot called for an early boarding due to an incoming thunderstorm. I felt relieved because leaving early would give me more time to make my connecting flight in Amsterdam. As everyone boarded, the clock started ticking. I eyed my watch anxiously, eager to leave the states.

With every passing moment, I glanced at my watch. A 10-minute wait became 30 minutes, and then 40. The pilot came on the PA system, announcing that a person had gotten sick on board. The employees down on the tarmac were trying to retrieve this individual's luggage. A wave of groans and scoffs echoed through the airplane. I couldn't help but think, *Come on. I need to get to Amsterdam. I can't miss my connecting flight.*

Another half hour passed, and we received a second announcement, informing us that the person's luggage had been found and we were ready for takeoff. The plane had not moved for over an hour, shrinking my 100-minute layover down to only 40 minutes. A few more agonizing moments passed. The plane finally detached from the skyway. We began moving towards the runway. *Amen,* I thought. After a few hopeful minutes of imminent takeoff, the plane suddenly stopped.

What now? I wondered. Five minutes. Ten minutes. The pilot spoke again, claiming that we were waiting for a spot to enter the assembly line of takeoff planes. By this time, the clouds for the thunderstorm looked quite ominous. Moments later, we were finally in the air. My 100-minute layover window was now down to 15 minutes. At least no lightning struck.

My heart pounded through the entire flight. I couldn't sleep. My mind was fixated on whether I would make my connecting flight. When we finally landed, I ran through the airport to catch my plane.

This journey in the airport included going through security, customs, and maneuvering around slowpokes.

My chest tightened as I heard a voice say on the PA system, "Last call for 11:00 AM flight to Berlin." I reached the gate, took a breath, and showed the attendant my boarding pass. I was so grateful the plane had not departed. The gate closed right behind me as I entered the skyway. Somehow my flight partner had gotten ahead of me—I still don't know how. Boarding my connecting flight, I felt elated beyond words. *I made it. The worst is over,* I thought. *Germany, here I come!*

This experience taught me the importance of keeping cool in tough situations. Traveling to a different country can be scary. Each one of us has our own tricks to calm us down.

Maturity and age has played a big part in how I handle situations. As a teenager, my mind was not ready for such a challenging task like air travel. As I got older, I became a new person. People age, mature, and hopefully adapt. If you choose to fly to a different part of the world, you will find yourself out of your comfort zone, and this will test your ability to cope in uncomfortable situations.

With my Asperger's, I cannot handle loud noises or crowded spaces. One time in Germany, I was crammed inside a train with dozens of other people. There was no room for movement and very little air to breathe. The heat from all the bodies added further to my discomfort. All I could do was close my eyes and imagine myself in a place other than a crowded U-Bahn.

You need to have control over your mind. Though you may have limits, you can train yourself to blot out unwanted sensations. This can take years of practice. I sort of adapted to big crowds and noises when I attended craft shows with my mother at age seven. She always told me to stay directly behind her and not let go of her hand. The thing that really helped me with these shows was enjoying the company of my mother as well as the event we were attending. These techniques helped manage the excessive stimuli I generally experienced in such situations. This worked because I was with my mom. Being with one person can make the difference. Focus on him or her, and then everything else turns into white noise.

Slowly expanding your comfort zone can be a benefit. I'm not saying you should run out and attend a live rock concert (unless you enjoy doing that sort of thing). Instead, take baby steps. If you have trouble with loud noises, turn up a stereo or an iPod just beyond your comfort level, so that you are able to handle the louder volume. To grow accustomed to crowded environments, try to participate in some events that involve lots of people. You don't need to run into a crowd—just linger on the outskirts of the event and slowly approach it. If it becomes too much, remain calm and back out. Doing these exercises over time can help you cope with loud and crowded settings.

Certain situations will be beyond your control. The only thing you can do is hope for the best. If you miss a connecting flight, find an airport employee and ask how you can arrange another flight. Look for flight attendants at desks or an information center. A missed flight only costs time; you do not have to buy a new ticket and start from scratch, although that might seem like the only option.

Airport kiosks can provide you with a list of alternative flights. When in doubt, check the kiosks. Call your folks at home to give them an update of your present situation. Doing this may help set your mind at ease. Talking with my mom or dad for a few moments always gave me a glimmer of hope for the next seemingly impossible task.

Your luggage can be lost. It is more likely to occur when you have connecting flights. That is why you should mark your baggage in such a way that you can easily identify it. Tying a red string on the handle or engraving your name on the suitcase will suffice. Knowing the brand of the case will help as well. When you go to baggage claim and don't see your luggage, flag down an employee and ask where you need to go for lost belongings. Or you can look for signs that lead to the lost luggage office.

Overseas Customs and Security

Leaving the states is easy, getting back in is hard. On my return trip from Germany, the security was tight, like an impregnable fortress. I saw several guards dressed in body armor from head to toe. A few were armed with automatic weapons. One guard had two handguns harnessed to his belt like a cowboy and two more strapped to his ankles. Needless to say, his firearm display was quite intimidating. Along with the armed security personnel were several different checkpoints each passenger had to go through in order to board the plane.

I was examined by multiple x-ray machines, ordered to set all my personal items in a bin, and cross-examined by a man in a suit. This sequence of events presented me with a level of airport safety measures that I've never seen. As a person with Asperger's, I did not have any trouble doing all the tasks the security personnel ordered. Every step was so structured and disciplined that the initial anxiety I felt about all the firearms dissolved. My mind was so caught up with completing the tasks that I no longer felt frightened.

The questions the man in the suit asked me were very direct and to the point. "What is your reason for the trip?" "What is your occupation?" "Are there any foods or items you are bringing with you?" I merely answered the questions directly and honestly. There was no thought to them. I simply knew the answers as soon as he asked the questions. While we talked, I instantly put to action the trick of mimicking eye contact by eyeballing part of the man's face. The acting and public speaking classes had certainly paid off.

The cross-examination with the guard ended quickly, and I was cleared to move towards the skywalk. A task I thought would be unpleasant proved very easy to accomplish. We Aspies are very meticulous, by-the-book people. If you think about going through security checkpoints like completing a recipe, you may surprise yourself on how well you do. Simply follow the instructions and move with the flow. That's all it takes.

First Note to Parents: Preparing Your Child for a Solo Journey

You can play an active role by helping your child with an autism-related disorder prepare for the journey. Work with him on the little things, like packing and booking flights. Arranging a flight itinerary can be challenging, especially when flying alone for the first time. Planning and acquiring connecting flights is tricky. If the task might be too daunting, consider contacting a travel agent.

It is vital that you educate your AS child on the unpredictable nature of flying. There are many factors that can make the trip stressful. You do not want the journey to trigger a meltdown. When looking for any connecting flights, make sure each layover is a minimum of three hours long. This will give your AS child some time in case a flight gets delayed or if she falls behind due to the long airport lines.

Reinforce any coping mechanisms that have worked for your child in the past—they may find them useful. For years, I worked with a yoga specialist. Now as an adult, I still find myself stretching my back and taking in slow breaths during frustrating situations. Most importantly, accentuate the fun your AS child will have on an independent trip. The air travel is only a fraction of the journey. The majority of it should be spent enjoying the new country or city.

Second Note to Parents: Traveling Abroad with a Class

If your AS child is a student and plans to participate in an overseas trip, there are many additional safety precautions to consider. Once your child is accepted for a study abroad trip, there are many forms that need to be completed. Review them with your AS child. It will help you and your child understand what the trip entails, the dates of travel, the fees, and so on. A school international ID is mandatory for study abroad students. Find out where your AS child needs to go to obtain one.

Insurance is also a requirement for these types of trips. When I got in contact with the travel agent for my Berlin trip, I paid for insurance in the event that I got sick or injured. Insurance companies are not universal—coverage in your home country may not work in another. Consider this option. The extra money might be worth it.

Finally, work out the flights so they match up with another student. Having a buddy is better for safety and navigating through the airports. Get in contact with the other student's parents and see about matching some flights. This may help reduce some of the stresses your AS child may feel.

For some flights, this might not be too difficult. During my senior capstone, I flew to California with a group of students. The teachers helped organize our flights. The college staff did such a good job that the majority of us were able to board the same flights and sit within the same seating areas of the plane. This may not always be the case. For my trip to Berlin, I had to arrange my own flights. Here are some important questions you need to ask. Will the school pay and organize the flight plans, or do the students need to find their own flights? This question needs to be answered early in your plans.

Chapter 17

New Surroundings

In continuation of the last chapter, I need to discuss the importance of adapting to new environments. The world outside your home is very different. The people and places in parts of this world could surprise, shock, or overwhelm you. Here I will give you tips and strategies to cope with these situations, with examples from two locations.

In a New Country

Every nation is unique. There are some basic guidelines for everyone to follow. Your native language may not be commonly spoken in the countries you're visiting. You will walk past people having conversations and not be able to understand a single word they are saying. Despite taking a year of German, the people in Berlin spoke so quickly that I could not comprehend their conversations. Every time

I ordered a meal in German, the server would reply to me in English. While I hoped to share their language, the native Germans knew I was a foreigner. My accent or poor pronunciations probably gave me away. Whenever you open your mouth, you give your nationality away. There is no way to avoid it.

Stick with your travel group. Do not walk the streets alone. Always have a friend, classmate, or colleague with you. A single tourist wandering around is an easy target. I would not recommend walking at night. Get a cab or assign yourself a nightly curfew.

This next tip is pretty easy for us Aspies. Do not engage in conversations with strangers, even if they appear friendly. I quickly learned in Berlin that homeless people tend to target foreign tourists. Every single day I was there, a man or woman would approach our group and ask if we spoke English. Each time, our answer was "Nein." Though the individuals seemed harmless, they were panhandling. Our tour guide explained that homeless people would entice foreigners into a discussion and then pickpocket them. This goes back to securing all your personal valuables. Remember the fanny pack? It can make the difference between keeping or losing your personal belongings.

Now for the next point. Do not wander off into the unknown. For people with Asperger's, this should not be too big of an issue, since we love structure and often avoid what we don't know. Nonetheless, this is a guideline worth addressing.

Do not publicly display expensive items. If you walk around with a smart phone, constantly taking selfies, or have a camera wrapped around your neck, you could make yourself a target. It's great to take photos—I captured many in Berlin—but don't always have your camera or phone out.

When in Germany, I adopted a repetitive process to care for my camera. I always brought my camera bag and tightened the bag's strap around my shoulder so I wouldn't misplace it. If I spotted something interesting, I stopped, took my camera out, and took a few pictures. When I finished, I put the camera away. As an Aspie, it was easy for me to adapt this repetitive ritual to protect my camera. I found this to be a good safety practice, because it is easy for me to get distracted, particularly in a foreign country where there are so many new things to take in.

Identify landmarks and street names that will help you locate your hotel. Since I have Asperger's, I am a very detailed-oriented person. During my Berlin trip, I noticed that there was a convenient store and a bakery on either side of the hotel. The hotel had a large flashing neon sign with red letters. I learned to use these details in case I lost my way. Retracing your steps can be a challenge. Have a map just in case, or look for a directions board. Many cities often have these available, particularly in the train stations.

My final tip for you is to remain self-assured and confident. I know body language is one of the many social cues that Aspies struggle to understand. Your gait and posture influences how others perceive you. Hold your head high, keep your chest out, and take deliberate strides. In this way you present an image of a confident individual. People usually don't pester those who walk with self-assurance. Walking in this assertive manner may also make you feel good about yourself.

A Meltdown in Germany

You may find yourself in situations that overwhelm you. When I was in Germany, I went with my class to a pizzeria for dinner. The restaurant was incredibly loud and full of people. We had to move single file to reach our table. Making matters worse, the table was far into the pizzeria and deep inside all of the commotion. I sat on an end seat, shoulder-to-shoulder with classmates—I had no personal space. I felt constricted. Everyone around me was talking, having a good time. All the voices and sounds blurred together. I could not focus on any one thing. On top of that, I was wearing a rain poncho. The heat from the jacket and other people made me feel flushed. There was no room for me to take off the poncho. I sat there, trying to keep calm.

Step-by-step, my mind began to shut down. I tried my deep breathing exercises. They did not work. I reached in my pocket and realized I did not have my iPod; I could not use music to tune out all the noises. I then tried to focus my attention to one specific detail in the room as an attempt to control what I was feeling. There was too much happening at once. I could not handle the situation. As I reached my limit, I slumped face first onto the table.

A pre-med student who happened to be sitting next to me came to my aid. He got me some water. Very quickly, our guide and a German student escorted me out of the pizzeria. I next found myself in a cab back to the hotel. The teacher returned to the restaurant while the German student stayed with me to make sure I was okay. The student and I sat in a little café and talked.

As an individual with Asperger's, I often have trouble expressing my thoughts to other people. That night, it wasn't a problem. The German student sat and listened to my words. I gave her some background about myself and shared with her my experiences as a person with AS. I was surprised that she did not judge me. Many people I have come across look at me funny when I mention a disorder like Asperger's. I guess they've never heard of it. This student immediately knew what I was talking about. In fact, she found the whole topic fascinating. She even mentioned the name Hans Asperger, the man who came up with the diagnosis. We talked for hours, enjoying one another's company.

As horrendous as my experience was at the pizzeria, this ended up being one of my best nights ever. I realized that I could not just rely on myself in certain situations. In Germany, I discovered the kindness of strangers.

Urban Settings

For many years, I hated the thought of traveling in a large city. Parades and social events often take place in streets, creating an abundance of bombastic sounds. Pedestrians disregard traffic signals and walk whenever they wish. Individuals drive their vehicles at erratic speeds and change lanes without turn signals. A city's population is a very diverse mix of ethnic, cultural, and socio-economic classes. This is not a bad thing, but it gave me a cultural wake-up call. Cities are chaotic and noisy, two characteristics that Aspies struggle to tolerate.

The crowding in large cities is also a breeding ground for crimes and accidents. Urban settings downright terrify me. The evening news always reports a person being mugged or injured, informing my mind that every city is a warzone. I remember driving downtown for the first time with my dad. I rolled my windows up and crept at a slow pace as other cars flew past me. I tried to comprehend it all. Attempting to identify and recall all the street names and locations frustrated me to no end. I couldn't filter out what was important and was irrelevant. It was too much to process.

I remember slamming on my brakes three times because either some fool pulled out in front of me or a pedestrian decided to jay-walk. *Why would a person jump out in front of me?* I wondered. *Do they want to be harmed?* I nearly panicked each time, fearing I was going to crash into someone. I gave my father quite a scare. From that road trip, I quickly made up my mind that I would never, ever drive in the city.

I had taken this hair-raising trip because I needed to locate a building for a summer internship. My father had agreed to ride with me. Because I felt uncomfortable driving in the city, I found alternative transportation. I researched bus routes to the downtown area. For three months, twice a week, I drove to a parking lot in the suburbs, paid for a bus fare, and rode the rest of the way. Fortunately, the final bus stop was only a block and a half from the company.

During that time, I became more confident and at ease with the new surroundings. My Asperger's mind eventually processed the new environment so that I could see the whole picture instead of zeroing in on a specific detail.

In fact, during my lunch I walked around the block, taking in different restaurants and buildings. I always stayed within a short radius from the company's location, allowing myself to take in one part of the city at a time. I began to realize that cities aren't so bad. You just have to adjust and know your way. Now, you may never picture yourself living, much less working, in an urban environment. However, millions of people are bound to a metropolitan area. Most likely, there will be times where you will have to travel in a city.

Driving in a City

City driving is entirely different from interstate or suburban driving. Roads usually only go one way. Lanes appear and disappear. Cars are often parked along the streets. Signs can be hard to read due to their diminutive size. Tall buildings are on all sides. The noise level is much higher. Do you see how processing all this information at once can be difficult? These few observations are a small portion of what you may encounter in a city block. Not knowing where you are going adds more stress. If you are commuting to school or work in a city, you must adapt to the environment.

To help curb the anxieties of this transition, I strongly encourage taking multiple road trips to familiarize yourself with the area. Bring a friend or a family member, preferably someone who has knowledge of the downtown district. On your first couple of rides, have a GPS and type in your destination. Do not panic if you miss an exit. I've done this many times, especially in an area that I don't know well. If you're on a two-way road, you can make a U-turn. Only do this if it's legal (some jurisdictions are uptight about U-turns). An alternative would be to drive until you find a parking lot or an area where you can pull off to turn around. If you're on the interstate, simply take the next exit and turn around. If you are using GPS, the route guidance will readjust to a different route or tell you to make a legal U-turn.

While you drive, don't just rely on the GPS. Look for street names, exit signs, and landmarks. After multiple trips in the area, you will become accustomed to the street names and will know where to turn. Once you have learned the downtown area, you will become comfortable driving in the vicinity and can understand the traffic patterns. Commuting to your metropolitan location several times can turn into a habit. As a person with Asperger's, I love repetition. The more I follow a routine, the less anxious and better I feel. Knowing the different routes and environments could make downtown driving an easier experience for you.

When driving in an urban environment, you must be watchful of everything. I have already mentioned that both drivers and pedestrians do not always abide by the traffic laws.

Remaining cautious can certainly help you watch out for such foolishness, but it does not guarantee that you won't have an accident. Pedestrians may not have the right of way, but you certainly DO NOT want to risk hitting a person. You could always blow your horn to warn them. This is an expected practice in the city. Do not be surprised when others do it.

Finding a Parking Spot in the City

Locating a parking spot can be an adventure (I say that with sarcasm). There are three places you can park. One is on the street. This is tricky, especially if you are inexperienced with parallel parking, and on-street parking is limited. Sometimes you can park near a parking meter and feed it with coins or a credit card. Once you deposit the money, you are given a limited amount of time to park there before the meter runs out.

Street parking is only meant for short-term visits. Meters only run for about an hour or two. Being an Aspie, I do not like the extra pressure of being tied to a ticking clock. It makes me feel anxious as I worry about how much time I have left before the meter runs out.

Do not rely on street parking for all-day parking. Also keep in mind that on-street parking is not very safe. Cars can be broken into or vandalized, even in broad daylight. This is why you should never leave personal or expensive items in your vehicle. If you must, hide them so they can't be seen.

The second option is parking lots. Cities have many of these available, and they are easy to access. However, there are two caveats. First, they fill up fast. Don't be surprised when you pull into one and find that there are no spots available. It is a first-come, first-served basis. And second, they are expensive. Downtown lots run on an hourly schedule. The cost is based on the length of time your vehicle is parked. You can quite easily spend $1 to $7 an hour for a parking spot. This is not an affordable strategy if you plan to drive to work or school every day.

The final option is garages. You can pay for them on daily, monthly, or (if you are enrolled in college) a semester basis. While they appear more expensive at first glance, they are the most practical for long-term parking. When deciding on which option to use, keep in mind how long you plan to stay at your destination and how frequently you are going to be there. Will you be there all day for work or a five-minute food carryout? Is this for one day or five days a week? When starting out, try a nearby lot or garage to see if it will work. During my second internship, I parked in a lot near the company. Later on, I discovered from a co-worker that there was a garage close by offering reasonable rates. When selecting parking options, ask a colleague for advice. Co-workers and employers can be wonderful resources in making your parking decisions.

Taking the Bus

Traveling by bus presents its own challenges. Buses are driven by strict schedules, and you are at their mercy if the bus runs late or breaks down. From my experience, buses often arrive early for morning commutes but are late nine out of ten times for evening departures. The hustle, bustle, and noise from the other passengers make a bus ride difficult for people with Asperger's. Earplugs do help, but where you sit also makes a big difference. I have learned that the best seating is near the front, away from the rear wheels and exhaust pipe.

The further back, the louder it gets. Since there is no assigned seating, seats fill up quickly. I made it a habit to arrive early before the crowd so I could get a better seat.

There is no guarantee you will get a seat near the front. In this case, you will have to endure the noisy environment. I discovered that buses have overhead railings for passengers to hold onto when all seats are taken. When a bus was packed, I stood behind the driver, gripping the railing for the entire bus ride. Though my legs ached some from standing, my ears felt better. It was worth it.

Another problem that comes from taking the bus is the crowded atmosphere, a by-product of public transportation. There is not much you can do if the bus loads up with people. Being an individual with Asperger's, I never liked being touched. As a young adult, I have somewhat grown out of this. I no longer shove or push people away when they touch me; this reaction is a no-no in the real world. Do not shove a person if he accidentally bumps into you. Very easily, this can grow into a confrontation and potentially even start a fight.

If a person bumps into you, alert that individual. Say something like, "Hey, you just knocked into me there." Often, you will get an apologetic response. If you do not receive a reply, leave the matter alone. You have said your piece. Most people do not intentionally crash into others on a bus. If you really feel uncomfortable with other people sitting near you, set an item like a backpack or a suitcase on the seat next to you. This only works if the bus is only partially full.

When seating becomes extremely limited, people find it rude if you're occupying two seats. In this situation, you have to make a compromise. This might be hard to accept, but giving up a seat will make it easier for you and the other person. While you may not want to give up a spare seat because it makes you feel secure, other individuals do not view it that way.

The last thing you need to consider is the cost. From my experience in taking the bus, I needed to have the exact fare. Credit cards and checks were not accepted. Before selecting a bus route, look up the costs. Find out if you can pay in cash or credit. You may want to look into purchasing a monthly pass. I only recommend this if you are commuting for full-time employment. If you are in the city for only three days a week, you will probably spend more on a monthly pass than on a daily fare.

When deciding to ride the bus, consider the costs. Determine if driving to work or taking the bus would be more cost efficient. Don't forget the intangibles of mass transit. On the bus you can sleep, read, listen to music, surf the Internet, and not have to worry about battling traffic.

Walking in the City

Whether you drive or take the bus, you will still have to do some walking. Remain vigilant and try to stick with a group of people when walking through the city. I know—we Aspies hate lurking around in crowds, but you will feel safer in a group. As I have clearly stated, urban settings are not safe. One person wandering alone in the streets makes an easy target for criminal elements. I'm not saying you have to travel with a large group of people; walking along with only two people would suffice. I felt scared walking alone when I made my first few trips downtown, but being among a group eased my anxiety.

As for handling loud noises, I recommend listening to music with earbuds. You may want to bring earplugs if the surrounding sounds are too overwhelming. Move away from the noise if it bothers you. Do not run into traffic to avoid them; this is dangerous and ill advised.

The only time you should ever cross the street is in a crosswalk and when you have the right of way. Sadly, people jaywalk all the time and risk getting hit by an unsuspecting driver. Sometimes you may find individuals who will approach you and say, "Excuse me?" or "Hey, you!" Other occasions, they might ask you for money. The best thing to do is ignore them and move on. This might sound like rude advice, but it could help you avoid an unnecessary confrontation.

Panhandlers make a living on other people's sympathy. Though it is always good to help someone out, you don't want to risk your safety for a stranger. Quicken your pace and move right past him. If you have to, run or maneuver around him. When in doubt, if you enter a part of town that gives you a bad feeling, do not linger. Get out.

Several years ago, my father and I traveled to New York City. We walked along the East River and ate some hot dogs. After our meal, the street vendors began packing up. Pretty soon, we were the only tourists wandering along the river as dusk fell. Cold chills ran down my spine as we quickened our pace to reach civilization again. It did not help that we ambled under an underpass decorated with offensive graffiti and a trash-strewn causeway.

We were in an unfamiliar and rather unsavory area. *We need to get out of here,* I kept thinking. In a matter of fifteen minutes, we were back on the main streets. Relief washed over us. This is a mild example of what you might encounter.

In addition to shady-looking characters, I would steer clear of groups of people who loiter around street corners. If you have to take a different route to evade them, do it. Do not approach or look at them.

The Brighter Side of the City

Cities are not to be feared. Yes, there is the out-of-your-element factor and the safety precautions you must consider; however, there are so many unique activities available in the cities. They have a variety of restaurants and stores you can visit. Being a passionate lover of food, I prefer walk-in eateries over a sit-down-and-have-a-conversation restaurant. Get a little fresh air. Visit a place you have not been to before. Explore a little and try out new things.

During one of my internships, I made it a habit to venture off with one of the company's employees for lunch. I learned to navigate my way and enjoyed some great meals. Exploring the city with a co-worker could make it easier than going alone. By the time my internship was over, I knew every restaurant within a square mile of the business.

Venturing out into the city will probably push you out of your comfort zone; it did for me when I tried the first few times. By the sixth or seventh time, though, I felt more at ease. Give it a shot. If you find that it is too much, then you know that wandering around the city is not your thing. Knowing your way and avoiding the not-so-great parts of the city does make a difference.

Note to Parents: Familiarizing Your Child with New Surroundings

Knowing how to get around in the city can help your AS child. Because of the loud, chaotic environment, I assumed that cities were giant mazes. As an individual with Asperger's, my anxiety goes through the roof when I become lost in an unfamiliar area.

The frustration of being lost in a city can be avoided with family road trips. Set a day or two aside where you can ride with your AS child and show him different ways he can travel to his new location. It may take a couple of trips for him to fully understand the area. Participating in one of these expeditions can also help you familiarize yourself with the part of town he will be working in.

Further instill in him the need for street smarts. There is always a risk of danger within a city. Roll the windows up, lock the doors, and leave no special items in the vehicle. Know that you can only help your AS child so much in this phase. The rest is up to him.

Chapter 18

Family & Emergencies

In my Asperger's mind, everything has to go according to plan. I don't like it when things disrupt my normal routine. Nonetheless, the unexpected always shows up. Accidents occur, loved ones get sick, and many other unwanted matters pop up. This chapter focuses on how to handle some of those unpleasant situations.

Dealing with Ill Health and Injury

I was taught that your health comes first. If you feel sick and know that going to work or class is not in your best interest, let your employer or professor know that you won't be there. It is common courtesy to notify your teacher or employer that you will be absent.

Missing one or two days because you're ill does not create a hopeless situation. As a student, you will usually have to make up the lost work. Contact the professor or a student in the class to obtain the assignments. If attendance is part of your grade, ask if you can do some extra credit to make up for the absence. This can be a possibility. Some teachers, though, do not give extra credit. In that case, you might suffer a grade penalty.

I had one professor who was so strict that, if a student missed a class, 5% of his overall grade was deducted. With my determined Aspie mind, I made it a habit not to miss his classes, even if I wasn't feeling so good. Through all my years in school, I measured my personal success through my grades. While not necessarily a bad thing, it became an obsession that was nearly impossible for me to let go. As my schooling went on, I grew out of this obsession. This began during a semester when I was enrolled in four challenging classes. I sacrificed study time for one class in order to do well on the other three. Even though I did not receive a perfect GPA, I passed all of the courses. Don't obsess over the little things. At work, if you miss a day, there is no makeup time. You may also forfeit pay for the time you missed.

If you develop a serious illness or a severe injury that will affect your performance either at work or school, this is when you need to have a sit-down talk with the person in charge. In my last semester in college, while working on a documentary, I sustained a bad injury. Just hours after we began filming, I was out of the game. The next six weeks involved surgery and rehab. I was prohibited from driving.

During the first few days, I felt like I had to withdraw from school. I saw no way to graduate as I had planned. Following the surgery, I made several phone calls to the school. The first one was to the department head. I spoke with him for a good while, weighing out my options. After we discussed my course load, he recommended that I push through and graduate on time. The next two phone calls were with my teachers. We decided that I would do my work from home and communicate with the classes via video conferencing. Except for the week of surgery, I did not miss a single class meeting.

While this situation was an extreme example, I learned an important lesson. Problems can be solved with the help of others; you don't have to do it all. There are ways to overcome issues, such as ill health or personal injury. If such an unfortunate thing happens to you, talk with your teacher. Most classes require face-to-face meetings. If an illness or an injury will set you back by a month or more, you may have to consider dropping the class.

The workplace poses a different situation. I had to take time off from my job because of a death in my immediate family. I called my supervisor and informed him of the situation. He was very courteous and told me to take as much time as I needed. I frequently updated him of the status and returned to work when I was able.

Family Emergencies

During my experience as a college student, both of my parents faced some life-threatening medical conditions. I remember driving to the hospital during my freshman year. My heart pounded for the entire trip. I entered the emergency room where my father waited for me.

He handed me a check for my tuition and said, "You don't belong here. Go."

Attending college helped me coped with these serious situations. I was fortunate enough to be enrolled in programs that centered on my intense interests. A second reason was because I still had my parents, despite their ups and downs. We worked together as a family.

Depending on your family member's health, taking a leave of absence from school or work might be necessary. There are two important things you need to think about. First, consider what is best for you. Staying at home and caring for a loved one may be right for you. I know what it is like trying to focus on a project when your mind is worrying about the troubles at home. Being there for my family has helped me.

The second thing to consider is whether a leave of absence will help your family. While living your own life is important, so is your family. My parents stressed that ideology for decades. Taking care of your immediate relatives can build a strong relationship. Because of my mother's illness, I have grown closer to my father. We are now at the point in our lives in which we do things together on weekends and work as a team on home projects.

Being an Aspie, it is very easy to become obsessed with a particular issue. I have found that sometimes it is best to be away from the situation to get your mind off of it. During my final two years of college, I stayed on campus five days a week, 10 hours a day. This 50-hour college workweek helped me cope with my mother's illness in ways beyond measure. I formed friendships, worked on projects with other students, studied for my classes, and even stayed late for some school-related events. While things grew bumpy at home, I did not take time off from school. I offered to drop out of college in order to care for my parents. They always turned down my proposal, urging me to finish school. I eventually fulfilled their wishes.

If you begin feeling depressed due to family-related problems, try sharing your thoughts with a close relative. Many times I have spoken with my parents about my concerns about their health. Sometimes it is easier to talk with someone else about it. I visited a therapist for nearly a decade. My discussions with him were kept confidential, and he offered an unbiased, third-person point of view. As you may guess, I also use exercise to help cope with my burdens.

Handling an Auto Accident

I had my first car accident two weeks after my eighteenth birthday. I clearly remember being in shock, yelling, and hyperventilating. Apparently, I called my mother and screamed into the phone, informing her that I had been in an auto accident. My mind swirled with wild, intense thoughts like, "What should I do?" "Is the other person all right?" Or worse yet, "Did I cause the accident?"

My second car wreck happened at a downtown intersection. After the collision, the only thought that entered my head was *get help*. Rather than staying put, I drove up a block to a gas station to get some assistance. Regrettably, this decision caused a lot of problems. As an Aspie, I have always coped with stressful situations by evading them, but driving away from an accident is illegal.

When you're in an accident, staying put is the only move you should make. Sit tight and call the police. Inform them that you have been in an auto accident. If you are injured, request medical assistance. Often good Samaritans may approach and ask if you are in need of aid. Respond honestly. These individuals are trying to help. Inform your family about your accident.

Once the police arrive, an officer will ask for your statement. Only you can explain what happened. Answer slowly and concisely. Avoid phrases like, "I think he pulled out in front of me" or "I believe she hit me." You must be clear and concise in your answers. Take your time and speak clearly. Recall every detail you remember. Do not try to deceive or think about what the officer wants you to say. As my grandfather used to say, "Mistakes happen, and you have to live up to them."

Have your license and proof of insurance ready when you speak with the officer. Talking with the police can be an intimidating experience, especially if your body is still recovering from shock. I have been taught that police officers are people you should not fear. They want to make sense of the situation and obtain all the facts for their report. Take deep breaths, close your eyes, and clear your thoughts. Such simple functions can calm your anxiety. I know these little tips are easier said than done, but try them out.

Exchange information with the other driver after the officer completes his report. Just know that accidents are quite literally just a bump in the road and they start as quickly as they end. However, the mental, physical, and legal issues can go on for months.

As an Aspie, I didn't become fixated on the accidents until later when I got home.

Note to Parents: Car Accident Repercussions

Depending on how much real-world experience your AS child has acquired, he may not be up to dealing with all the issues of an automobile accident. You may have to play an active role. I ended up in court for both of my car accidents. These were nerve-racking experiences, neither of which concluded in anyone's favor.

People can be mean-spirited and uncooperative when it comes to declaring who's at fault. The worst in people can arise during a stressful situation like a car wreck. It could fill your AS child with anxiety and lead to depression.

Following my second car wreck, I recall driving to class with a tight chest and an upset stomach. As I reached the college garage, I bolted to a trash can and retched. I got sick all over my clothes. Later, I visited a bookstore where I purchased new clothing, hoping to remove the stench.

Adding insult to injury, the insurance companies held my car hostage, leaving me without a vehicle. The only safety net I had was my parents' love and guidance. To help settle both the insurance and damage claims, we hired a lawyer. It took time, but we got through all the red tape and settled.

Hopefully, you and your AS child will never have to go through such a hassle. If this happens, sit down with your child and ask him to share with you all the details of the accident, what he saw, and what he said to the police. From there, choose your next course of action. Be rational and supportive of your child. I cannot tell you exactly what route to take. Each accident is unique. Try to work it out with the insurance companies first. If necessary, you may have to seek legal counsel.

If the traffic case does go to trial, you and the attorney will need to prepare your AS child. Wear nice clothes. Go over speaking strategies and limit answers with mostly "yes" or "no" responses. Cover as many facts as possible, and do what you feel is necessary to help your AS child out of a traffic jam (no pun intended). An auto accident will be a learning experience for your Aspie child. Having been in three accidents, I have learned more of what not to do versus how to react.

Epilogue:
Final Notes

I hope the tips and experiences I have shared might assist my fellow Aspies in their endeavors and in pursuing their future goals. The world is a huge place. There is plenty of room and opportunities available for all of us. Only you can make your future. Anything you set your mind to do is possible. Nothing can hold you back. Fulfill your dreams, but also know your limits.

As an adult, I still have difficulty with loud noises and crowded environments. This became apparent when I attended my best friend's wedding reception. Sitting quietly alone in the ballroom, I watched as hordes of people poured inside. Hundreds of voices spoke and laughed at once. Worse, the band performed loudly in the background. All of the sights and sounds caused me to face sensory overload. With only a small ounce of clarity, I packed my belongings and left the room. It was so overwhelming that I began hyperventilating.

Depending on where you are on the autism spectrum, you may or may not be capable of handling situations like these. This is why you need to go out and explore. Doing so will help you learn what is within your comfort level and what is not. You have to find your way. If a rock concert is not your thing, then don't go to one. Keeping away from certain elements that may trigger a meltdown is an ongoing process. You learn what you can tolerate, but you have to at least try. My father often told me, "Live life to the fullest of your abilities."

Note to Parents: Your Child Can Be Destined for Great Things

I am not the same person I was years ago. As a teenager with Asperger's, I could never picture myself within a city environment. Now, in early adulthood, I have done what I considered the impossible: flying across the Atlantic Ocean and back, earning two college degrees, and working full-time. Your AS child can achieve many such things, and he will need some help navigating the different phases in his life.

As I have made abundantly clear in some of the previous chapters, do not coddle your child. He has to learn to do things on his own, otherwise he will be stuck at home. The hope is for him to move on. If your child is more severely burdened with autism, this may not be in the cards. In that case, you will need to find an alternative strategy on living accommodations that fit his needs.

Call me naïve, but I think with the right care and treatment, your Aspie child can do anything he wishes. I have come to accept my Asperger's as a gift instead of a burden. This perspective has not only changed my outlook in life, but also my desires for personal, educational, and career success. This positive mindset will set your

AS child on the path to wonderful accomplishments. Encourage and prod him towards victory. You may be surprised what he achieves on his own.

Acknowledgments

During my sophomore year of college, I remember thinking that this would be a great book to write. I was not yet ready to write it then, because I had a lot more to experience in life. Four years later, directly following my college graduation, I decided to broaden my scope, adding work and travel tips to the original idea. Within the five years of publishing my first book, I have met some very influential people who contributed greatly to this work.

This book would not have been possible without my parents. My mom and dad set time aside to help me with my drafts. They are the most amazing parents an Aspie child like myself could have. They have not walked a mile in my shoes, they've run an entire marathon!

The next group of people I need to thank are four of my college professors, under whose direction I have studied. It is unfair to rank them in any order; each individual is unique and has introduced me to new ways of thinking:

Kevin Burke is one of the best professors any college student could ever wish for. Aside from his general kindness and honesty, he sets more time aside for his students than any other teacher. He saved my life when I broke my arm in California. If it were not for his presence, Lord knows what may have happened. I not only see him as a great mentor, but also as a wonderful friend. Many, many thanks to you, Professor Burke!

David Hartz is the most unique professor I have ever had in the classroom. He pushed me further along than most teachers, making sure I performed to the best of my abilities (and then some!). I received a wealth of creative knowledge from him. I recall many times when I met with him outside of class hours, inquiring over design or aesthetic-related questions. He always welcomed my visits. Thank you, Professor Hartz, for being patient with me on all of my assignments.

Jay Petach is simply a fun teacher. Always full of energy and enthusiasm, he knows how to create an enjoyable learning environment. The fact that he works with his students on class projects is truly wonderful. I never felt afraid to raise my hand. Many thanks go to him for his hefty contributions to my capstone project. In all honesty, I feel that I would not have done as well without his guidance and assistance. Thank you so much, Jay!

Of all the professors I had, Ted Ferdinand is the one who most poignantly taught me that "the sky's the limit." Creativity and fun have no boundaries. Those are the two most important things I learned from him. Like the other few great teachers I've had, he is willing to bend backwards and throw lifelines to his students. Ted, you exhibit the characteristics I like most about professors—brilliance and compassion. Thank you.

Another group of people I have to thank are the hardworking folks at W-CET Cincinnati. Everyone there feels like an extended family. The producers, editors, sound artists, and videographers exposed me to so much in the public television industry. All of you guys and gals are great! And finally, I give thanks to Future Horizons for giving me an opportunity to release this book for my fellow Aspies. Wayne and Leta, thanks for making the "sequel" a reality!